PRAISE FOR TARA JAYE FRANK AND *YOU ARE BEFORE THE WORLD*

Tara Jaye Frank reveals that what applies to the workplace is true in all the places we work: living rooms, offices, nurseries, halls of power, the great outdoors—any space where we strive to make our marks. Hers is a voice of experience, vulnerability, grace, and grit. As a result, *You Are Before the World* offers strategies of clearheaded optimism, self-loving boundaries, and an ever-expanding love of the world, including everyone who calls this blue planet home.
—TAYARI JONES, NEW YORK TIMES BEST-SELLING AUTHOR OF *AN AMERICAN MARRIAGE*

You Are Before the World is a beautiful reminder that beyond titles and accomplishments, who we are is rooted in what we believe, how we love, and what we're willing to give. This book brings you back to what really matters—with heart, depth, and intention.
—MINDA HARTS, BEST-SELLING AUTHOR OF *THE MEMO*

This book is transformative. It literally moved me to say the no I needed to say.
—ELAINE LIN HERING, *USA TODAY* BEST-SELLING AUTHOR OF *UNLEARNING SILENCE*

This isn't just a book. It's a reckoning, a remembering, a permission-giving return to self-love that doesn't require performance.
—LORI HOLT, RECOVERING CORPORATE EXECUTIVE AND FOUNDER OF THE WOMEN'S WEALTH COLLECTIVE

You Are Before the World is raw and honest and carries a luxurious depth that makes it impossible to put down.
—DR. JADE SINGLETON, DIRECTOR OF NINETY-TWO AND FOUNDER OF IKONI COLLECTIVE

When your one life holds many—parent, professional, pioneer, peacemaker, public servant—you need reminders of your right to be both giver and receiver, benefactor and beneficiary, lover and beloved. With piercing vulnerability and genuine heart, *You Are Before the World* offers this and more.

—Dr. Sheila Robinson, founder, publisher, and CEO of Executive Woman Media

TARA JAYE FRANK

YOU
Are Before the
WORLD

You Are before the World by Tara Jaye Frank
Published by Tara Jaye Frank
2450 Lakeside Pkwy Suite 150-130
Flower Mound, TX 75022
tarajayefrank.com

This book or parts thereof may not be reproduced in any form, stored in a retrieval system, or transmitted in any form by any means—electronic, mechanical, photocopy, recording, or otherwise—without prior written permission of the publisher, except as provided by United States of America copyright law.

Copyright © 2026 by Tara Jaye Frank
All rights reserved

Visit the author's website at tarajayefrank.com

International Standard Book Number: 979-8-9926812-1-5

While the author has made every effort to provide accurate internet addresses at the time of publication, neither the publisher nor the author assumes any responsibility for errors or for changes that occur after publication. Further, the publisher does not have any control over and does not assume any responsibility for author or third-party websites or their content.

Author's Note: This book tells my personal and professional story. It reflects my present recollections of experiences over time. While some names and characteristics have been changed, some events have been compressed, and some dialogue has been recreated, it is still my truth. I stand by every word.

Photography: Kendra Swalls
Styling: Roxanne Carne

26 27 28 29 30 — 9 8 7 6 5 4 3 2 1
Printed in the United States of America

To me,

*and to you—
conditioned to forfeit your dreams,
fix everyone's problems,
and fall back so others can fly forward.*

*May this book inspire you
to reclaim your selfhood,
clear a path to possibility,
and keep making a difference in the world
without losing yourself to it.*

CONTENTS

Prologue: Out of the Darkness ix

Part I
YOU: Be Still and Know

1. How Do We Steady This Vessel? 1
   Minding Your Mind 1
   It's Time for a New Story 9
   We Don't Have to Fight to Exist 13

2. It's Time to Look Deeper 21
   Stand on Values, Move With Belief 21
   Desperately Seeking Humanity 27
   Creating a New Vision 31

Part II
ARE: Take Care of Yourself First

3. How Do I Choose Myself? 43
   Sometimes All You Can Do Is Hold On 43
   Through the Fire 49
   Navigating a New Season of Darkness 52
   Knowing When It's Time to Let Go 53
   Getting Off the Cross 54
   Honoring the God Winks 57

4. Say Goodbye to Self-Sabotage 59
   You Can't Keep Being the Good Person 59
   Take Up All the Space 62
   Tending to Your Wounds 65

5. Restoration 71
   You Have to Accept What Is 71
   Get Clear About What Matters 76
   Do What Counts 82

6. Getting Free 87
   Setting Limits 87
   Say No to People Pleasing 91
   Stay Out of Grown Folks' Business 96

    Let Them Use Their Own Brain 100
    You Are Enough 102
    Tighten Up Your Boundaries 104

Part III
BEFORE: Clear a Path for Others to Follow

7 Emerging 111
    Expanding Your Territory... 111
    Stand on Your Rock 116
    Ditch Perfection 118

8 Growing Up.. 124
    Be Disciplined 124
    Do What You Gotta Do—For You 128
    Trust the Process..132

Part IV
THE WORLD: People Are More Important Than Systems

9 Leading Through the Wilderness 141
    Creating Safety... 141
    Interrogate Your Reality.. 149
    Seeking Alignment 153

10 You Have to Start With the Heart................................... 158
    Build Bridges..158
    Sit Down, Be Humble 161
    Be Willing to Be Wrong About People 167

11 Learning to Believe Again 175
    Stay Woke... 175
    It's Time to Claim Your Inheritance 180
    Keep the Faith 186

Afterword: A Hope and a Future.. 193
Resources... 194
Acknowledgments 197

Prologue

OUT OF THE DARKNESS

For he chose us in him before the creation of the world.
—EPHESIANS 1:4, NIV

THERE'S A SACRED SPACE between leaving it all on the field and opting out entirely. The former takes every ounce of faith and fire in your bones. The latter is sometimes the only thing you can do to stay sane—to keep the fear of being abused, rejected, diminished, discarded, or stripped bare, again, at bay.

I don't remember a time when I didn't feel afraid. My godfather loved to recount the afternoon he walked into my bedroom to find two-year-old me standing in the crib, having just awakened from a nap. He spoke to me. I smiled. And then he yelled for my parents: "Come quick; she's delirious!"

Apparently, I didn't smile much. My family jokes that I was a mean child. I now know that what others saw as lukewarm indifference was always fear. Fear of strangers as a toddler became fear of being misunderstood as a schoolgirl, which turned into fear of rejection as a high schooler, then fear of failure as a young adult entering the workforce, and finally, as a young mother and wife, fear of pain, abandonment, or loss.

My ever-present fear earned a name when I was twenty-five and pregnant with my first child. I'd made an appointment with a psychologist because I couldn't sleep. My breathing was chronically shallow. I was caught in a relentless thought pattern of "what-ifs" about my baby, my marriage, my work...my life. And one day, while driving home from the office, I believed I was having a heart attack. In what felt like an instant, I couldn't fully inhale. I rolled the window down and gasped for air. When my lungs would not inflate, my throat began to narrow, I started sweating, and my body shook. Two days later, I sat awkwardly in a fluffy beige chair across from a stout Black man with kind eyes who diagnosed me with generalized anxiety disorder. Generalized anxiety disorder is a clinical term for feeling like there are butterflies ever alive in your chest.

I've learned to manage my anxiety over the years, but it's always there. I tend to worry more about mortality or injury than other people. I'm prone to overthinking when in conflict with someone I care about. I still throw my foot at an invisible brake in the car passenger seat if a driver, usually my husband, makes a sudden move. In an unhealthy state, when I'm stressed or not sleeping well, my brain works against me, imagining the worst possible outcome in almost any potentially dangerous situation. It makes my neck hurt and my shoulders ache. It tires me.

These days, when it feels like the very fabric of society is in tatters, the fear is ever present. It seems we're all suffering with generalized anxiety, if *generalized anxiety* means a foreboding that follows you everywhere you go.

The last time I'd watched election night news, I'd endured four years of chronic stress. The 2016 Trump presidency changed me molecularly. My anxiety had reached new heights of terror, and my patience a new low. Every careless statement and dehumanizing act sent me into a tailspin. It was during this period that my husband gave me a new nickname: Angry Mommy.

Throwing paper towels at US citizens? *Angry Mommy.* Going on about how your ideas are the best-ever ideas in the history of best-ever ideas? *Angry Mommy.* Turning one of the most important positions in the world into a bully pulpit? *Angry Mommy.* Downplaying the pandemic while people died in hallways waiting for emergency treatment? *Very. Angry. Mommy.*

I was always on edge, waiting for one unhinged slight to send me plummeting into the abyss, during which the anxiety spewed in compound curse words and creative insults. Being an empath is good when it's good and excruciating when it's not. Not a day passed between November 2016 and November 2020 that I didn't long for an abrupt end to what I saw as an existential threat to our shared humanity: myopic self-interest. I hoped it was a blip we would learn from then course correct with our future choices.

I celebrated Joe Biden's win in 2020 not because I was especially excited about Joe Biden as a candidate but because it meant I could stop panic-watching the news and reading ominous headlines from the fifty-eleven media outlets we'd grown accustomed to. I was glad for a return to normalcy and welcomed boring news cycles with open arms. I observed, tentatively at first, then with slowing breath, as Biden brought our collective heart rate down. *Thanks, Joe.*

When I settled into my living room recliner to watch the presidential election results roll in on November 5, 2024, I felt genuinely peaceful. I believed America was ready to turn the page—from divisiveness, vitriol, and antiquated ideas to something more hopeful and unifying. We were now an increasingly diverse nation with an accelerating climate crisis, growing global conflict, eroding civil rights, and a resurgence of white nationalism that had been conquered in 1865, then again in the 1960s.

Inspired by Jotaka Eaddy and Win With Black Women, democracy-loving people of every stripe gathered on web calls and in stadiums all over the nation to support Kamala Harris, the vice president of the United States and first woman-of-color nominee for president. Just three months prior, she'd walked boldly into the space created by Biden's choice to step down and had run an admirable campaign. She was focused, measured, and outcome oriented. She shared policy ideas to fuel small business growth, lower health-care costs, lower barriers to entry for home ownership, and strengthen our educational system. She vowed to protect women's rights and civil rights for every American. Kamala: *For the People.*

Not all Democrats were happy about her track record or her stated position on the converging global humanitarian crises, but compared to her opponent, I thought the choice painfully obvious. Every speech painted an optimistic picture of who we could be. Each rally was an enviable party. Election Day turnout was record breaking, and enthusiasm for Harris was through the roof. We would surely wake up the morning of November 6 with a renewed sense of goodness and mercy. And I hoped it would follow us, if not all the days of our lives, at least for the next four years.

I sat down in the living room recliner with my election night accessories: celebratory snacks, a blue mocktail I made from a recipe I found online, my emotional support animals—a ten-pound Morkie (Maltese and Yorkie mix), our Doberman, and our goldendoodle—and my phone for live-posting. My heart was beating fast—in a good way.

But it became evident early in the night that something was off, meaning incongruent with the results that were expected and that I personally wanted. Red mirage? I didn't know. I went to bed early because with each state prediction, my anxiety spiked, and I wasn't sure I could withstand the emotional roller coaster. In fact, I was sure I could not.

I pressed play on my favorite sleep music, let our dogs outside one last time, brushed my teeth, washed my face, and climbed into bed. I slept horribly. Occasionally, I'd see the light cast from my phone, indicating either a text message or news alert, and I fought the urge to pick it up. *I don't want to know. Not yet.* My stomach was in knots. I turned over, pressed my pillow to my face, and had a good cry.

Please, God. Have mercy on us.

I was trying not to mentally review all my fears about another

Trump presidency, but they scrolled erratically through my brain like an old, silent movie: National abortion ban. A (re)resurgence of hate crimes. More gun violence without controls. Mass deportations with no consideration for children or families. Challenges to women's fundamental rights. Adverse impact on our global allies, leaving them vulnerable and untethered from the nation they'd come to rely on for support. I knew things would get bad for many Americans, but also that they would get exponentially bad for those of us who'd be unrepresented in this newly elected administration. When I woke Wednesday morning, I learned there was no red mirage—just a sobering red reality. *God, no.* And: *God, why?*

I was numb. I lingered in bed, trying to calm my nervous system. Finally, I swung my legs to the side of the mattress and slid my feet to the floor. Every step I took was like moving through molasses, as if the connection between my brain and my body had been cut. My husband was out of town, and while he's usually the first person I go to when faced with anything unpleasant, I considered his absence a gift. I felt submerged, and I knew that in his infinite practicality, he'd struggle to understand the depth of my despair. A few friends I texted said they felt peaceful. Others were rallying to fight. And some acknowledged the gravity of the situation while choosing to focus on what they could control.

I thought, *What is wrong with these people? This country is about to become unrecognizable to us! Do people not understand how bad this will get?*

I decided I would detach from media. I sent a few emails, stared blankly at my computer for a couple hours, and listened to gospel music on repeat to remind myself that God was still real.

I FaceTimed my mother. She gave birth to my oldest brother three days before Martin Luther King Jr. was shot. She lived through a dark time in this nation and survived it. *Would we?*

"Hi, Mom."

"Hi, Tara Jaye. Unbelievable," she said, shaking her head.

"That's one word for it," I scoffed. "Mom, you were a young adult in the sixties. You lived through a time when people were trying to send Black and brown folks back to oblivion. What was that like?" I needed proof of life.

"I was in my twenties," she said. "It was hard. We just took one day at a time."

She didn't say much more, and I didn't know if it was because she didn't remember or because she didn't want to think about it. The significance of her being in her twenties weighed heavily on me, because while I had enough concerns of my own, I was acutely worried about our six young-adult children. I felt both angry that this was the society they must navigate and guilty that I was fortunate enough to mature during a relative reprieve.

Later that day, our oldest son, Abram, came downstairs to the living room and plopped in the chair across from the one I was slumped in, where I sat staring at the floor, fixated on a thread unraveling from the carpet. *I am that thread—thin and wiry and sticking out like a sore soul.*

I knew Abram didn't believe in our existing government structure. He felt it wasn't people-centric and that it was destined to fall apart so something better could take its place. In this moment, with fifteen feet and almost thirty years between us, it hit me that he may have been the wise one all along.

We made small talk for a few minutes. Then he asked, "How are you doing, Mom?" It was a formality. He knew the answer.

I took a deep breath and removed my glasses, which I'd slid on out of habit. Our children are adults, so I don't pretend with them anymore. I told him I was sad and angry. I told him I knew this outcome was possible but genuinely believed we would choose differently. I told him I was sorry that this is the reality he and his siblings and their peers must contend with when they should be dreaming and daring with abandon. And then I uttered the words that got caught in my throat for what felt like eternity before pouring out in a flood of sobs:

"My optimism. It's gone."

I couldn't access it. It's hard to explain, but it was like looking for your car keys in the place you always leave them, except they're not there. And you have no idea where else to look, because this is where they belong. I've always been able to take a hit, reframe, and come back swinging. My body, however, was limp. My heart, shattered. I stood up slowly, as though I might stumble, and shuffled to the hallway bathroom to grab some tissue. I'm aware, even as I type these words, that all of this sounds extremely dramatic. And I want to say to you, unequivocally, it was.

"It's okay, Mom," Abram said. "Maybe now we'll remember what really matters. Maybe now we'll start relying on each other again."

I glanced up from the pile of damp tissues growing in my lap. "What do you mean?" I asked sincerely.

My goldendoodle, whom we named Cassius Clay when he joined our family during the pandemic, appeared concerned. He kept resting his humongous head on my leg, then sitting up straight in a huff, then resting it there again so I wouldn't miss the point he was trying to make: *I'm here*. This sweet gesture usually cheered me up. Not today.

"I think the answer is local," our son said. "Neighbors. Colleagues. Family. Friends. The barista at the coffee shop. The trainer in the gym. People we see and know and can connect and build with." And then: "The answer has always been us."

He looked at me with such compassion. It struck me in this moment that this child among our six children—all beautiful and brilliant—was the most comfortable with my tears.

I used to be dismissive when he would say such things. Not

because I didn't believe him but because everything is—in some way—political, and to not participate seemed naive. Today, he sounded omniscient.

"Maybe, son," I said. "Maybe."

Back on social media, the "We must keep fighting" memes were everywhere. Personally, I was tired of fighting. Black women are notorious for doing invisible work—things that need doing but are not noticed or celebrated. In this election, the vast majority of us voted for mutual care and collaboration, but more than seventy million people did not. This harsh reality made me feel invisible, disrespected, devalued, and unprotected. My relationship with America wasn't perfect before, but now it felt irrevocably broken. I felt aimless. *Where do we go from here?* For many of us, the answer was simple: home.

As someone who identifies as a helper, it's never been my nature to wallow. When I feel hurt, I allow myself time to grieve, to rage, and to momentarily detach. But ordinarily, I don't stay stuck. I'm a creator. When I find myself in an undesirable situation, I create. This time, I was struggling.

The darkness was already rolling across our land in a myriad of ways: in plans to deport tens of millions of people (whether their families were American citizens or not), in texts telling Black youth in various states to report for slave duty, and in posts threatening to rape women using the hashtag #yourbodymychoice. This was about so much more than my preferred candidate losing an election. It was about legitimizing and legalizing our worst impulses. Hatred disguised as pride was being resurrected as a way of life. I felt disillusioned, as did many Black women who voted for character, inclusion, hope, health, and unity while far too many people voted for racism, sexism, or cheaper eggs. *Who have we become? And how did we get here?*

I had a flight to catch that same night, and while I was looking forward to the authors' retreat scheduled months before, I was anxious about traveling through crowds to get there. We were aware that our timing was risky, but we thought we'd be celebrating. My airport experience was awkward and stressful. I peered at every person who was not Black and female with skepticism: *Was it you?* A silent, lonely war, with no clear markers to confirm whom I was fighting alongside or against. I put on noise-canceling headphones and looked down at my phone from the time I hit security to the moment I landed on the other side. I didn't want to see or hear anything that might threaten my composure. I was extremely fragile.

I arrived at our family beach home before the others and ordered groceries to be delivered. When the driver's name populated in my app, I chuckled. *Socrates.* The car pulled up a few minutes early, and out climbed a brown-skinned man with curly black hair and a medium build. He had kind eyes and looked to be in his mid- to late thirties, but he was probably older. *Black don't crack.*

"Is Socrates your real name?" I asked when he reached the door.

"Yep. The name my parents gave me," he replied, with a tone indicating that this conversation was not new.

"I could use some philosophy right about now," I said, only half-jokingly. A subtle plea.

"About what, exactly?" he asked. *Did he not know?*

"The world," I sighed.

Without hesitation, he replied, "You are before the world." He then handed me my bags, took the customary photo for evidence of delivery, and walked away. I stood motionless in the breezeway, letting his words settle on me.

When I shared the brief exchange with my author sisters, so much came up for us:

Take care of yourself first. *You are before the world.*

You must clear a path for others to follow. *You are before the world.*

People are more important than systems. *You are before the world.*

I later found a Bible verse with the same sentiment: "For he chose us in him before the creation of the world" (Eph. 1:4).

I couldn't stop thinking about what Socrates said, and I wondered whether he knew just how profound it was. How timely. How needed. The following days brought increasing clarity, and everything I'd learned and taught over the years about focusing on what you can control, doing what you can with what you have, and leading from where you are began converging in my mind. I knew I couldn't let myself drown in helplessness. But it was also true that I couldn't see my way out or through just yet, and I was convinced that doing so would get harder in the months and years to come for all of us—even many who thought they wanted this.

My author sisters and I had a beautiful weekend. We cried, we laughed, and we ate amazing food. I cooked for them and allowed myself the simple joys of doing every individual thing mindfully. Sautéing. Braising. Simmering. Plating. Garnishing. Arranging. Cleaning. Putting things back in place.

Meanwhile, Black women who rode hard for Harris were sharing memes about getting off the "change the world" ride for good.

I'm done trying to save people who don't want to be saved.

Listen to Black women, or don't. It's whatever.

You can find me at home, minding my business and drinking my water.

Friends were sending me videos and articles via text and online with inflammatory headlines. I ignored them at first, then asked them to stop, responding with multiple variations of the phrase "Thanks for thinking of me, but I'm not consuming media right now." Some seemed unpleasantly surprised when I rejected their attempts to commiserate with me. But my misery didn't need company. Honoring myself in this moment meant a lot of things. It meant accepting the range of emotion that grief carries while admitting that this was, in fact, what I felt: grief. It meant seeking solitude when I needed it. It meant telling people what was really on my mind instead of saying what they expected me to say.

I was determined to feel my feelings for as long as necessary. At the same time, I wondered what we would do after we processed our pain. I've never known Black women to stay down. Would this time be different? Would we refuse to throw ourselves back into the helping arena? Would we really watch from the sidelines when help was needed and not provide it? I didn't believe so. I was also aware that it wasn't just Black women who voted for progress. According to Pew Research Center, 75 percent of Black men did too, along with 79 percent of Jewish people and millions of people from other groups. I usually felt compelled to be inclusive—to make room for others' hurts to rest inside my own, but I didn't have it in me.

And still, even with the walls erected by the national repudiation of Harris, here's what I knew for sure: Helpers can't *not help*. Healers can't *not heal*. Givers can't *not give*. Doers can't *not do*. We—those who plant seeds of change and spend considerable time and effort watering them—would want to once again make a difference without being depleted. I knew we would need to reimagine helping in ways that didn't wound us. This middle ground wasn't just about resting. And it was far more than positive thinking. It was something else: a new way to show up for us and others that wouldn't leave us naked and afraid.

On the way home, the creative ideas began flowing, and Proverbs 18:16 came to mind: *A person's gift makes room for them.* I still felt heavy with hurt, but my creativity was pulling ahead in the race, showing me, in vivid color, not only how I might reset my baseline but how I could help others in the process. This book you're holding or listening to is the result of that epiphany.

You Are Before the World is a humble offering that redefines the pursuit of balance as a deeply personal voyage. In it, I share my own restoration story and the many practical ways I've learned to sustain myself as a helper in a world that needs *so much help.* Like you and countless others all over the world, I desperately want to be of use without being used. To give generously and still have something to hold. To love and be loved in return. To do good and not be undone. To have, if not a life of ease, a life in harmony.

This book is a call to discover—then expand into—the coveted space between "all" and "nothing." Through my own sometimes painful but profound revelations, you may feel more encouraged and equipped to view yourself, your circumstances, and the world around you as fertile ground for hope and possibility.

You Are Before the World explores, with great candor and clarity, the helper's dilemma: *When giving is your calling, when do you not answer the phone?* It also provides instructive inspiration and paradigm-shifting perspectives, but there are no guarantees—because for every good thing I've learned and gained, the battle continues.

You Are Before the World offers an inside-out view of my own life in motion and, as such, is not a chronological tale. Instead, it unfolds from the depths of me with lessons I've learned about taking up space in my own life. It illuminates choices I've made to honor myself by releasing what no longer serves me and by thinking differently about both challenges and opportunities. It is not about politics, work, or any other societal structure—but it does interrogate the ways these structures seek to diminish us and paints a portrait of a sometimes private, sometimes public resistance.

The journey of *You Are Before the World* begins with how I was navigating the world after the 2024 election and includes lessons like when to hold on and when to let go, releasing harmful constraints, deciding what matters and investing in what counts, how to be content, and establishing limits.

It unpacks ways I learned to draw parameters around my life—both hard lines and dotted ones—so I can do the work I'm purposed to do without getting lost in other people's wants and expectations of me or in my own head.

And finally, *You Are Before the World* delves into helping beyond my own sphere—in companies and communities—in ways that allowed me to cultivate connection across differences and inspire change from within so more of us can make a difference in the world without losing ourselves to it.

Ultimately, this book is an invitation to embrace the divine promise of "a hope and a future." We are the promise. We are the hope. We are the future. We—with our feelings, needs, and purposes—are *before* the things we do, the gifts we give, and the achievements we earn.

People often say there are three sides to every story: my side, your side, and the truth. In this book, I share my life experiences through my lens because that's all I have. Others may have experienced these moments differently. But this story is mine. And if you consider yourself a helper, I believe you'll discover that my story—at least in part—belongs to you as well.

Filled with hard-earned wisdom, practical guidance, and permission to be, *You Are Before the World* will soothe your soul, strengthen your spine, and provide loving reminders and the real-world ammunition you need to honor yourself while living, loving, and leading a life of significance.

PART I

YOU

Be Still and Know

Dear Reader,

Do you feel untethered?

Do ideas, people, and places that once grounded you no longer feel aligned?

Are you reflecting more about your work, your purpose…your life?

Is there a quiet knowing emerging in you that while you're not yet who you will be, you're not who you once were?

This part's for you.

Chapter 1

HOW DO WE STEADY THIS VESSEL?

Minding Your Mind

A FEW SHORT WEEKS AFTER the election, I boarded a plane to Florida, poised to sink into my seat of choice—the window—where I always do one of two things: marvel at the clouds on a sunny day or monitor them on a stormy one. The forecast called for rain, and I'd already begun mentally preparing for mild turbulence. I say the same prayer every time I fly, inspired by my friend Myron, who went full preacher mode on a turbulent business trip once.

"Steady this vessel!" he called out loud and full-throated. "Lord Jesus! Put your angels in front of the plane, behind the plane, above and below, to the left and to the right, inside and outside! Put your angels in the cockpit and in the aisles! Bless the pilots and the flight attendants!" The people around us averted their eyes, and while I also hate turbulence, Myron's unintentionally public performance distracted me from it.

I can still see him all these years later—eyes tightly shut, hands gripping the armrests so hard his fingertips turned white, and his large, muscled frame stiff as a board. When the turbulence stopped, we laughed for a long time. It wasn't funny, but it was hilarious. I've never told Myron his prayer comes alive every time I board a plane—in my quiet voice, of course.

Back on the Florida flight, a tall, white man who looked to be in his late sixties or early seventies was poised comfortably in the aisle seat, reading a book.

"Excuse me," I said politely, and he stood to let me by.

"I like your shoes," he offered. Shoe compliments were common since I started wearing a hybrid sneaker heel invented for professional women on the go—or, in my case, short people who stopped wearing regular heels post-pandemic.

In routine fashion, I removed the noise-canceling headphones from my travel bag, placed them on my head, settled into the seat with my laptop open, and began to write. After five minutes or so, he asked me what I do for work. It had been a long week. I'd just returned from facilitating a working session with a client in St. Louis and was looking forward to a relaxing weekend by the beach with my husband. But I didn't want to be rude. *Nice girls talk, even when they don't want to.*

"I'm an author and a consultant," I responded with a smile—a mental override to the annoyance of being interrupted.

"What do you write and consult about?"

I couldn't tell if he was genuinely curious or just making small talk.

I paused to consider how to answer his question because I sensed one of two things would happen: either he would nod while uttering some pleasantry and go back to his book or I would end up in a two-hour debate disguised as a conversation about the value of my work.

"Leadership," I responded, aiming to keep things simple for both of us.

"Oh, yeah? Me too," he chuckled. "Not really, but I founded a company, and I do lead people."

I asked a few follow-up questions, and in his response, he dropped: "I voted for Trump; I'm not sure if you did."

"I most certainly did not," I reflexively shot back, not meaning to be curt but clearly unable to help it.

He laughed. *What was so funny?* I wondered. *My comment or me?*

"So how do you define leadership?" he asked.

I took a deep breath and decided to use this time—during which I couldn't escape even if I wanted to—to learn something about him and his worldview. I thought twice, but curiosity propelled me forward.

"I believe leaders are responsible for unleashing talent fully, freely, and fairly to drive business results," I said, pausing for emphasis. "Some people consider that DEI. To me, it's just what great leaders do."

I smiled confidently and let it simmer. I knew I'd opened a can of worms, and they immediately began squirming. His facial expression looked as if disdain and apathy had a baby.

The rest of our conversation was all over the place. He opined that DEI was unfair, and I asked what he thought it meant. His understanding was that it meant giving unqualified people jobs just because of their race or gender. I told him that what he described is illegal and that while I understood how his oversimplified view was the narrative being peddled, DEI is most certainly not that. He took exception to my narrative comment, clearly sensing what I didn't say, which was: *I know you heard that on your favorite news channel, but that's an alternative fact.*

To bolster his argument, he offered examples of times he's witnessed unqualified people get jobs because of their race. I clarified that unqualified people get hired every day for reasons other than merit, like nepotism, for instance. It doesn't mean the foundational work associated with DEI is unfair but that some have applied it unfairly. Then I raised a few examples of visible (read: government) positions being populated by friends and fans of the current president and asked if he considered that merit-based hiring or DEI, according to his definition. He averted his gaze and changed the subject.

Maybe I shouldn't have bothered to continue, but I went on to explain each letter—*D, E,* and *I*—in ways I hoped might illuminate the true nature of the work, because acronyms, as we continue to see, are woefully insufficient and easily weaponized.

"Diversity allows companies to benefit from varied perspectives and experiences," I said. "It expands our vision and ensures we can remain relevant to as many people as possible into the future. It makes room for multiple realities."

He was still listening, so I kept talking. "Equity is not about giving unqualified people an edge. It's about balancing the scales that have been imbalanced for generations by ensuring everyone has equal access to the insight, resources, and opportunities they need to be successful. It means everyone has a shot to get the job and that they're fairly compensated when they do.

"And inclusion is leading in ways that acknowledge, invite, trust, leverage, recognize, reward, and support all people, making sure every person feels part of the team and can contribute to outcomes."

I felt proud of myself, but he liked his explanation better and seemed disinterested in anything that might challenge his beliefs. In whole, our discussion touched upon a lot of topics: the lack of generational wealth for brown and Black families due to racism in hiring, housing, and banking; whether poverty is the result of poor choices or an institutional design; America as the land of opportunity or not, and for whom; and—most profound in my eyes—independence versus interdependence. He valued the former, and I, the latter.

At least a few times during our conversation, he said, "This might sound racist, but . . ." Many more times, in response to my attempts to address his false equivalencies, he replied with a dismissive and deceptively simple "I just don't care." It was a pleasant enough conversation on the surface, but I was disheartened—not because his perspectives surprised me. (Trust me, I've heard it all.) I was disheartened because once again, it made me question whether we can survive what I see as our most profound illness as a society: the complete lack of consideration or care for people beyond our front doors, the blatant and unabashed self-interest.

My story about the state of our nation toward the end of 2024 had already begun to form, and my verbal dance with this airplane stranger didn't help.

We're doomed.

Nobody cares about anything or anyone but themselves.

I can't do anything about it.

People who love me suggested I think positively. They encouraged me to move beyond my feelings and be reasonable. I wanted to scratch their eyes out. I was still grieving, and they were asking me to skip over the grief and jump to the lesson. *What lesson? That half of America cares more about money and power than about people?* They thought I was catastrophizing. In my mind, I was simply being a realist. *This is bad. And it's going to get worse.* For weeks, that was the only story I could see, and in my opinion, any other interpretation was wishful thinking.

Even as I believed my story to be true, I was acutely aware that ruminating on it for too long could be dangerous. Every time I repeated my story to myself, the darkness got darker and the light, harder to see. There's a point in this sort of painful repetition when you ask whether you should bother. But you know that when you stop bothering, you get stuck. And when you get stuck, you grow resentful—toward people you blame for your circumstances and toward yourself for being unable or unwilling to overcome them. It's a vicious, counterproductive cycle that had me by the wrist. And I was certain—from scores of posts, calls, and texts—that my resigned mental state was duplicated in the hearts of millions of others, especially Black women, in America and beyond.

Within days after the 2024 election, an AI-generated version of original artwork by Navi' Robins, which depicted a few Black women gathered on a rooftop watching the world burn, was making the rounds on social media. Navi' spoke on Instagram about the work Black women put into Harris's campaign and expressed his concern that we would be most harmed by the result. I felt the spirit of the image: *I tried to help you. You didn't want to be helped. I'm going to stop trying.* But I knew that sentiment wouldn't last. Not for a lack of discipline, but for a lack of conviction. No one I knew genuinely wanted to stop caring. We were just so injured that caring felt untenable.

I thought back to an evergreen tool I learned from Debora McDermed of the Vertical Dimension during my Hallmark years called "The Belief Cycle." It suggests that what we think repeatedly becomes a belief and that what we believe carries emotion. When we're unaware of our emotions or fail to question the thoughts behind our feelings, we behave out of them. And when we do that, we influence our results. I never forgot this concept, and I've shared it with many professionals since—not to deny how external factors impact our realities but to help people understand that the stories we tell ourselves affect how we show up—or don't—when it matters most.

I needed, even if for my own saving, a different way to think about what was happening to America and in Americans—a story that would allow me to continue being myself and doing my work and making whatever difference I could wherever I found myself. Not a fantasy but a frame that made room for healing and left space for growth.

Lunch with a colleague just before Christmas would prove insightful. We met at a member organization event almost ten years prior. She grew up in a conservative family and was married to a conservative man but felt abandoned by the Republican Party. She was having a hard time identifying the "family first" and "rule of law" spirit in the party's current iteration and voted according to her values, which in 2024 were more aligned with Harris than Trump.

I told her my airplane story and how discomforted I was by this belief about conservatives that was taking root in me: that they only cared about themselves. It's a horrible thing to think about a massive group of people. I knew this, but the signals kept signaling and I had yet to find convincing evidence to the contrary. While I tried to conceal it, there was skepticism in my tone—an unintentional and uncontrollable "prove me wrong" energy.

She could have gotten offended and shut down. I was talking about her loved ones, after all. But her rational nature prevailed in the moment, and for that I was grateful.

"Maybe it helps to look at it this way," she began. "You believe that we're all interconnected—that if I do well, you do well, and vice versa. I believe that too, but they—the people who voted for him, the ones you think don't care—don't believe that. They believe in individual freedom. For them, this is less about not caring than it is about personal responsibility."

I mulled her reframe for a bit, trying to reconcile the two ideas. It made sense in theory, but I was struggling to understand how prioritizing personal responsibility led so many to discard their fellow citizens. Even in this thought, I could feel how deeply committed I was to my story—that people on the other end of the political spectrum did not care about human beings beyond their front door. That they were willing to throw them away. What's worse, this belief was giving rise to a similar mindset in me: *I'll just focus on my family and let everyone else fend for themselves.* It sounded good but didn't feel good. Was it true that seventy million Americans didn't care about anyone but themselves? I asked myself how believing this was helpful to me or my work.

To challenge my frame, I recalled every word and phrase I'd heard uttered by conservatives as a contrast to liberalism over the past several months: *Liberty. Freedom. Merit. Choices. Work ethic. Opportunity. Independence. Individualism.* I forced myself to consider their opposites, thinking it might help me perceive the problem differently: *Subjugation. Captivity. Inferiority. Control. Laziness. Adversity. Dependence. Collectivism.* I had to admit that, save collectivism, the descriptors didn't sound great. If I believed the paradigm was this black and white, I might bristle against liberalism too. But the former ideas are not real—or at least not that simple—for those who've been relegated to the margins of society. Our aims were more complex, and our lenses more expansive and inclusive. For us, this was not about contrast. It was about saturation.

For example, our response to liberty is not subjugation but liberty *for all*. Our response to freedom is not captivity but financial, psychological, spiritual, and bodily freedom *for all*. Our response to merit is fairness *for all*. In most cases, it's an opening—not an alternative—we seek.

This mental exercise reminded me of what I already knew:

People who've never been disadvantaged based on race, gender, ability, country of origin, or sexual orientation tend to believe that their achievements are of their own doing. They don't recognize the invisible advantages that connections, socially acceptable characteristics, and generational inheritances provide them. They think every good thing that happens for them is to their credit and that every bad thing that happens to another is to their shame.

The caste-based threads woven throughout societies are unseen and unfelt to people who've never tripped on one while traveling toward a dream. And I knew, from research and firsthand experience, that to ask people to see the invisible is a tall order.

So, which is it? Are they cruel and unusual? Are they blind and ill-informed? Or are they simply watching another movie on a completely different channel? I wasn't clear, but I knew that my story about them—or at least the mass-generalized version—only reinforced my hopelessness.

A reframe was in order, for my own benefit and for the benefit of the leaders I serve who hail from all backgrounds and claim varied belief systems—one that made the rift less about pure politics and more about awareness, care, and connectedness. More about what happens in us than around us. More about what we could accomplish—together—with big ideas, open hearts, and willing hands, but in ways that didn't demand anyone's silence or complicity.

It's Time for a New Story

In December 2024, having just watched another well-made but pain-provoking film, I posted that I didn't want to see any Black "struggle movies" for a while. I wanted to cozy up on my couch with marshmallow-topped hot cocoa to watch us dream dreams, fall in love, find joy, repair frayed parental ties, and learn life lessons the hard way but not the traumatic way. I wanted a new seat from which to witness our shared experience, where I could be entertained without personalizing every act of aggression. *Wicked*, for example, was a beautifully reflective film—*and* it hurt to see a young, powerful, visibly different girl be vilified her entire life, then manipulated, and finally targeted when she refused to succumb to a diabolical plot. *Relatable*.

Black women are the sacrificial lambs of our time, and when Elphaba flew off on that broomstick and declared her freedom because "Everyone deserves the chance to fly," millions of us knew what it meant. She would be free—but also lonely and misunderstood for the rest of her life. I found this moment in the film both exhilarating and exhausting. I shed a few tears in the theater, much to my great niece Amia's bewilderment, because I knew exactly what Elphaba was giving up and why. And it was far more consequential than the chance to be de-greenified. There's always a *yet higher* calling, and Black women—along with others who've been chronically disrespected—are conditioned to answer. Our empathy is forged in each slight, in each moment of suffering.

This is the tightrope every helper walks: whether and how to split the difference between too much fight and not enough, and what's worth sacrificing in the battle.

"I don't want it. I can't want it...anymore."

For as long as I've been a witness and for years before that, the strength of Black women has been constructed atop a shared burden. We've been planting flowers in dry ground while holding our collective breath on the other side of *still*: A bad thing happened, and *still*...A person disregarded me, and *still*...I earned the opportunity, and *still*...

This deeply ingrained legacy of overcoming is something I feel both pride in and great resentment toward. I reflected on every example—public and private—where Black people I know and don't know have responded to disrespect with saintly calm. When Angela Bassett lost the 2023 Academy Award for Best Supporting Actress and showed visible disappointment, the internet was ablaze with criticism, as if it's unnatural to want to win and be sad when you don't. When the world fears your dismay, any hint of it creates waves of alarm. This is what it means to have your humanity universally denied.

Yes, we are resilient—*and* we deserve to come to joy, peace, achievement, love, and support with ease the way others have and do. Why must we *overcome* as a prelude?

The struggle is real and relevant, especially now. I've been reflecting on the long-term implications of our response to this moment in time. Our psychological ties solidify more intensely when we feel persecuted than when we share a common hope, and common hope is hard to cultivate in chaos. It needs foresight and planning and reinforcement to take root, to grow. When life comes at you fast—and keeps coming—it feels impossible to step back long enough to seed hope. With every post, article, or example of near and present danger we share, we are bonding. And when we use chaos as glue, we make it stick. Sometimes I think we're afraid we'll lose each other without it.

The chaos is all around us, but I don't want it anymore. I don't want to breathe it in. I don't want to create it. I don't want to serve it to anyone. I don't even want to validate it, which is difficult to do in a negative news cycle that won't quit.

What I wish for is a new story. I want to find you in a place where the soil is fertile and the "stills" are fewer. A place with common hope. I want you to find me there too. And I pray that we can cling to each other long enough to get there.

I am, in no uncertain terms, holding two seemingly opposite things in my hands: our right to feel the very real pain of each transgression and our need to transcend it so we can live our remaining days as we deserve—gracefully. But that means revising our relationship with struggle. And I'm not sure we feel open to that quite yet. That story is deeply ingrained, and those of us who've studied the history of race and gender in America know that the arc is long.

The beauty of attending a historically Black women's college like Spelman College, where I attended, is the specificity with which you learn about the Black femme experience. We didn't have Black History classes. We took classes like Violence Against Black Women in the Media and Original Art Works of the African Diaspora. No surface gliding. No generalities. All depth and nuance.

Thirty years ago, I sat in literature class as Spelman professor Judi Gebre-Hewit taught an eager group of young English majors a lesson on leveraging oppression. Because of her insights, her phrasing, and the tone of her voice, I hung on her every word. I'd never heard the term *leveraging oppression*, but she described it as elevating our suffering above another's to place ourselves on higher moral ground.

"We leverage oppression by making ourselves feel more righteous," she explained. "More deserving of empathy, consideration, or reward—because of the extent to which we've suffered."

According to Professor Gebre-Hewit, having suffered more can make us feel superior. I'd seen this attitude surface everywhere, including in my own thinking. And while I felt it was true that we'd suffered more, I occasionally asked myself how this translation served me. *If* it served me.

I've reminded thousands of professionals over the years that just because a story is true doesn't mean it's helpful. A true story is based on facts and real occurrences and might end there. A helpful story emerges from the truth and supports forward movement. It has enough stretch for us to believe in something useful. It invites us to imagine what harmony feels like and to envision what role we might play in creating it. It shifts our energy from blaming a person toward naming the problem or, in some cases, the opportunity.

The true story for many in America and in other parts of the world is that doors to freedom and opportunity, and therefore peace and prosperity, remain shut tight. But a helpful story is that there's always a window. Through that open window, we can notice the places where the breeze flows in and the times when the sun casts just enough light on our faces. We can make appointments with like-minded people in those places and at those times. And we can see that no matter how dark things may appear, we are still the viewers—the protagonists. We have the power of choice, and the ending is—at least in part—in our hands.

These days, open windows look like asking myself "What else could it be?" when I witness problematic behavior out in the real world. It's not about giving undeserved grace; it's about regulating my emotions and lightening some of the latent rage I carry. People are often unaware of our unique life experiences and the ways those experiences make life difficult for us. And—at the same time—they do not always wish us harm. Conflating the two made me feel lonely and perpetually on guard. Whether I'm right or wrong is irrelevant if I condition myself to suit up either way.

And still, I hold the pen. I'm not obligated to include everyone in my story. A week after my conversation with the airplane stranger, my husband and I saw him at the airport. I pretended not to see him. He pretended not to see me. I was fine with that.

WE DON'T HAVE TO FIGHT TO EXIST

It took time to realize that I'd been conditioned to let people talk to me crazy under the guise of "healthy debate." When you regularly experience microaggressions or subtle acts of exclusion, it can feel like looking through an old pair of glasses—you're not always sure you see what you think you see.

My expertise has been doubted, even when my years of experience far outweighed that of the one doubting it. My feelings have been challenged, as though a person outside of my body can define what's happening inside it. After a while, you stop questioning the questioner and begin questioning yourself. *Am I sure? Is that fair? Did I read that right?* So you do more research. You ask more questions. Sometimes you construct entire exchanges in your head, formulating all the responses you wish had been accessible in the moment of offense.

It's important to distinguish between disagreement, which helpers must learn to navigate with curiosity and respect, and disrespect, which no person has the obligation to tolerate. Sometimes we feel disrespected when others don't mean to disrespect us, and I'm not advocating for defensiveness here. But when someone comes at you with negative energy and you express concern, a well-intentioned person will get curious. If they insist on being negative, it's fair to challenge their intentions.

In the summer of 2024, I published a post on LinkedIn about the senseless murder of Sonya Massey, a Black woman who'd been shot three times by an officer with a bad track record. It was an acknowledgement of the sadness many Black women were feeling at that time.

A stranger entered the chat. "What did you hope to achieve?" he wrote.

I responded that I was empathizing and that if he quickly reviewed the many thoughts left by Black women who appreciated it, he might understand. A tense exchange erupted in the comments section between him and other Black women, which resulted in the commenter private messaging me with a challenge to publicly debate him, coupled with an assertion that if I declined to do so, he would take it as an admission that I couldn't defend my position. He ended his note with, "If [you don't want to publicly debate], have a nice life."

I was filled with rage. I drafted a few responses but deleted them all and chose to block him instead. My initial instinct was to defend myself because that's what I've been conditioned to do—prove myself, my intelligence, my integrity. But then I began thinking about the disrespect he felt so comfortable wielding against me, and I resisted. A stranger tried to put me to work that day, and I noticed this as an insidious pattern of attack against many of the helpers I follow on social media.

When California was ablaze with multiple wildfires, people from all walks of life jumped into action—sending money, arranging donations, offering room and board, and sharing information that might help people find safety and recover. Helpers were helping, even in their helplessness.

It didn't take long for the "cause police" to jump into inboxes, shaming people for posting about anything but the burning. They didn't do this to everyone—only to those who reliably speak up on critical issues and who periodically share their lot: money, books, information, time. *How dare you talk about [x] when there's still fire? You should use your platform to help with the fires. What are you doing about the fire?*

Many helpers had been posting nonstop about the fires since they began and were doing what they could to support victims. But it wasn't enough, and this reinforced my personal experience that once people see you as a helper, they behave like you belong to them.

It's not "strong" to share space with people who abuse you. We're not expected to suffer indignity and call it power.

In the summer of 2024, the National Association of Black Journalists invited Donald Trump to their annual conference in Chicago. Many Black journalists and members of the organization dissented, warning that his past behavior and views on race should disqualify him, but the interview went on as planned. In a span of thirty-four minutes, Trump questioned Kamala Harris's racial identity, claimed migrants were going to take "Black jobs," and outright disrespected the journalists on stage. At one point, he grabbed a bottle of water from the small table beside *ABC News* reporter Rachel Scott, attempted to drink from it, then set it down on the table nearest him when he couldn't get the cap off. It was, according to people on both sides of the political aisle, a disastrous interview.

Some Democrats gloated because the interview revealed in their opponent a lack of clarity and control that reinforced their narrative. Republicans tried to minimize the damage and move on from it. But those of us who respect journalism as a profession and Black journalists as professionals were saddened. We felt that harm was given a platform in a space designed to uplift and celebrate. I wondered how the team behind the event reconciled this moment for themselves—whether they got what they hoped for. Or more. Or much, much less. The trade-off was unclear to me, and at the same time, I strongly related to the tension that exists between doing your job (or what others perceive to be your job) and preserving your peace. This is a tension I hold daily in my work.

Shortly after the war broke out in Gaza in October 2023, I read a post that snatched me by the throat. The violence was at a fever pitch, and innocent people were being maimed every day in places normally considered safe, like schools and hospitals and homes.

The post was written by a woman whose work I greatly admire. She was clearly angry—not just at the situation, but at the many people she expected to be more outspoken about the escalating atrocities. Her post was a bold accusation. To paraphrase, she said: *Anyone who works in diversity, equity, and inclusion who is not doing and saying more about the war in Gaza is cowardly at best and a fake at worst.*

It's difficult to put into words the way this made me feel. It was a mixture of shame, empathy, and annoyance. I'd posted a prayer for those hurt by the conflict but had stopped short of condemning any specific person or group.

In the same span of time, people on American soil were being violently targeted as the enemy, and this enemy differed depending on the lens. Palestinian friends and supporters wanted me to put a stake in the ground about the genocide in Gaza and believed my failure to do so conflicted with who I claimed to be. Jewish friends wanted me to speak out against the violence against Jews in America and felt let down by what I didn't say or by what I said too gently. Both cohorts made assumptions about my beliefs regarding the situation and concluded that I didn't care enough about them, their people, or their causes.

This made me feel sad but also frustrated because I never claimed to be an expert on foreign relations—only a person who believes every human being has a right to visibility, respect, value, and protection. My realm is the workplace. In fact, through the years, I've been very clear about a few things related to the work of diversity, equity, and inclusion—namely, that while it's true that a handful of practitioners pioneered the work that is now DEI, I generally don't believe in DEI experts.

Diversity, equity, and inclusion is an extremely broad and sometimes ill-fitting moniker. It often encapsulates every single talent and leadership system, process, behavior, and metric inside a company. It also includes multiple systems, processes, practices, behaviors, and metrics outside of the company. To say one person is an expert in consumer branding, product development, talent planning and advancement, leadership expectations and accountability, business strategy and operations, research and data science, innovation, community building and relations, social justice, and local, national, and international labor law... it's just not real. And yet being associated with the work—even when it's not the whole of what you do—automatically brings a mountain of expectations to your doorstep.

I sat with other people's emotions a bit, then crystallized in writing what has always been true for me: *I despise violence. I pray for peace. I care about humanity. I believe that those most at risk need our love, support, and protection. I think we have lost our way—that power and greed are winning the day and that it will take conscious intervention and thoughtful resistance to turn this tide. I will do what I can, when I can, and how I can to make the world a better place.*

The truth was I didn't know enough about the war and its contextual history to say much more than the above. In my private time, I did more research. I spoke to people not only about their experiences, but also about their feelings surrounding what was happening. I asked what they needed most. I delivered work inside companies helping team members feel heard and respected, and I created spaces where they could disagree without disparaging—where they could care and be cared for without abandoning their sense of responsibility to fight for what they believed in.

Personally, I had to come to terms with who I am as a helper and be clear about who I am not. I'm a leadership and culture consultant who knows a lot about what employees need and want at work, the practical ways leaders can meet those needs, and how to equip and encourage people for progress. This includes vision and strategy, research and data, leadership and culture alignment, skill building and practice, interpersonal savvy, bridging expertise, talent process enhancement, and systems of accountability. This is my realm. Nothing more, nothing less. And because I never claimed otherwise, I determined I would not allow anyone to use me as a weapon in the thought-leadership wars they felt called to wage. It's not reasonable or fair. In fact, I got so comfortable with this boundary that I started blocking people I caught trying to provoke me and my followers by tagging me in their controversial posts.

Months later, I opened LinkedIn to find that a woman had reposted something I wrote for and about Black women. Attached to her post was a diatribe about me being a hypocrite for not also talking about other groups who were being persecuted. This is the day I knew I'd successfully embraced my boundary. I gave her a piece of my mind, then blocked her. No second chance to talk to me crazy.

Resisting in this way requires accepting a few realities: *People will think bad thoughts about me. People may try to ruin my reputation. I may turn some people off. I could limit my opportunities.* These outcomes don't feel good, but what feels worse is overexerting yourself to meet others' demands simply because they might mischaracterize you if you don't. When I experienced mischaracterization during my divorce, a friend who'd been through the same cycle told me to just keep being myself. She said my actions would eventually overshadow the accusations. This advice sustained me when people I loved were dragged into manufactured stories. And it would sustain me now.

We—those who help, heal, support, and encourage—deserve a middle ground. We want to save the vulnerable *and* be in community. We want to empathize with others' pain *and* experience joy. And we want to stand up for what's right without anticipating the knockdown. You can shine a light on darkness without becoming the flashlight people shine on their agendas. This is the evolution tale we need to tell first to ourselves, then to each other—one that fills the pages between giving our all and being left with nothing. *You and me before the world.* And when we can embrace our own complexity—boundaries and all—it will be easier to embrace the same in others.

My road to resistance was paved by the hard, cold fact that I cannot be everything to everyone. I will continue to bring my best to any space I occupy. It's not always everything I have, and it's not always everything people want—but it will be my best available in the moment. If I can't do that, I won't show up at all.

Going before takes courage and grit, but it doesn't have to take you out. Do what you can with what you have when you have it. And when you can't, for reasons you may or may not want to explain, don't. It's that simple. It has to be. We can only ever do our best.

Chapter 2

IT'S TIME TO LOOK DEEPER

STAND ON VALUES, MOVE WITH BELIEF

I WAS AT A MEETING in Washington, DC, when, in answering a question about the declining state of politics, a Black CEO distinguished between unintended and intended consequences. This spoke to me because I believed the broad-based anti-inclusion movement was strategically constructed and executed—that it had less to do with fairness and more to do with stemming the momentum toward balanced leadership and equality.

The positioning of DEI as a form of reverse discrimination had taken root in the minds of many white men (and some white women) who believed the changing demographics of America would leave them behind. It winnowed huge swaths of work down to a single idea—race-based hiring targets—and outright rejected the inconvenient truth that the workplace has never been merit-based.

From a psychological perspective, the wholesale rejection

made sense to me. I didn't agree with it, of course, but I understood it. To see meritocracy as a fallacy gives way to another, more troubling idea: that some have attained position and power for reasons *other* than merit. It's a hard pill to swallow, and one historically disadvantaged people have been poisoned by since America's inception.

This positioning, which effectively tainted the long-standing pursuit of fairness, made way for a coordinated attack on Black women in the workforce. As I put the finishing touches on this book, over three hundred thousand Black women have either been forcibly removed from their jobs or indirectly pushed out by more sinister means—chronic disrespect, abject cruelty, exhaustion, or mental and emotional distress. In five short months, Black women's unemployment skyrocketed from 5.4 percent to 6.7 percent. While we were devastated by the fallout, none of the Black women in my circles were shocked. This is exactly what we predicted would happen. It has always been true that those on the edges of society feel the pain of harmful policies and practices first and most.

The work has never been about advantaging some and disadvantaging others. It's about opening the playing field so that all people, along with their unique experiences and perspectives, can contribute to making our work and workplaces better for everyone. I believe the root cause, while unconscious for some, is about fear of loss.

In the game Chutes and Ladders, the chute is the slide that gets you to your destination faster and with more ease. It's the shortcut. The ladder is the way of hard work. It takes longer and carries more risk. No one wants to lose use of the chute. That would mean having to climb the ladder—or worse, being forced to share the chute. This is what I watched post-election: people kicking us off the ladders we'd been methodically constructing and climbing, while safeguarding the chute. The bully tactics that have historically allowed people to keep what makes them feel important—money, power, and prestige—were alive and well. And some were upholding these cruel and self-obsessed behaviors as symbols of strength.

In early 2025, my friend Keith texted me with a link to an article about the gap between anti-DEI law and the rippling corporate response to the law. There was considerable air between the two, but corporations were overcomplying, the way you might double the time to stop when following behind a car or run from a fight so you don't get hit. *Better safe than sorry.*

"I get it for those who have huge government contracts," I responded. "They have no choice. They're beholden to stockholders and can't afford to lose half their revenue. But the companies who don't *have* to do this and are obeying in advance? Ugh."

He shot back with one line: "Because this is what they wanted to do anyway."

I didn't want to believe that, but I knew he was at least partially right. I imagined all the corporate leaders who felt coerced into diversity, equity, and inclusion initiatives. Who reviewed the data, read the think pieces, and felt that doing nothing would cause more noise than doing something, so they threw us a few bones: A person or two responsible for thinking about the work. A relatively small budget. Agreement to "support" a set of actions that made some people feel really good and others feel not too bad. Now that the tides were turning, it was as good a time as any to throw in the towel. There were so many towels being thrown that whatever negative media attention they might earn would be dispersed and probably wouldn't last long. This is the bet they were placing. Classic risk-benefit scenario.

When you never saw the work as an extension of your values or you never believed in the business benefits of more and differentiated ideas, greater company loyalty, and a caring, connected, and collaborative workplace, the whole bolted-on effort was easy to discard.

There were harbingers of anti-DEI stickiness well before the election. A few years ago, I had a conversation over breakfast with a friend who was a president in a multibillion-dollar technology company. In a moment of extreme frustration, she asked if I could help her understand the disconnect between her CEO's expressed value for people and equality and his absolute resistance to legitimizing initiatives that might help employees succeed in more equitable ways.

"I don't get it," she huffed. "How can someone so successful not see that what he says is important and what he's willing to prioritize don't match?"

She shared how this conflict made it hard for her to walk the company line: "I hate this kind of dissonance. I don't agree with his position, and I feel disingenuous trying to explain to my team why we can't do what our employees are asking for. If he doesn't really care about people, he shouldn't say he does." She'd written him off as a fake.

I explained that while her CEO may *value* equality, he may simultaneously *believe* that equality already exists inside their workplace. And if he believes equality already exists, he won't feel compelled to try to achieve it. To add dimension to the point, I shared that some who enjoy significant privilege are extraordinarily passionate about equity initiatives that benefit the poorest among us but do not see their own employees—who may not be hungry or homeless or otherwise destitute—as needing the same added investment that might balance the scales in their environment. Aligning themselves with those they see as destitute soothes their conscience without threatening their position. No one who needs help with food or housing will get anywhere close to the throne.

After my brief exchange with Keith, I reflected on how

hungry I was for the truth in all its forms. If a company leader doesn't believe diversity is a strength or that fairness matters or that including people from all walks of life enhances workplace culture and makes work not only more enjoyable but more productive, I didn't want them to pretend they did. I wanted them to do us a favor and roll back their promises. I wanted to know what they really value. And what they really believe.

People joke about meeting a "representative" when they start dating someone new, meaning the person is on their best behavior and says all the right things. But when it comes time to show they care, to give something up—time, talent, energy, or convenience—they backpedal. In the same way, while many companies had put on a good show, it was becoming clear some had little to no intention of staying the course on issues of fairness and inclusion. That was their prerogative, of course. Contrary to the administration's posturing, private companies have a right to invest as they see fit. But as is true in all my relationships, I wanted to know the real them: The promises they keep when there's no praise to be had. The way they move when no one's looking. The short-term gratification or convenience they're willing to exchange for long-term value.

As naive as it may sound, I maintained this position even as the pressure became fiercer and the capitulation list grew longer. Even as PBS got defunded, universities got sued, and media professionals—like Joy Reid from MSNBC, Stephen Colbert from CBS, Jimmy Kimmel from ABC, and Karen Attiah from *The Washington Post*—were targeted for doing their jobs.

I started seeing diversity, equity, and inclusion rollbacks as a necessary reveal. If I only had so much time, talent, energy, and money, I wanted to spend it in alignment with my values. The revelations helped me by illuminating the companies whose leaders *do* care. In my estimation, they were the ones risking something to put people first. They were standing on their values and moving with belief. They were staring down the fire and withstanding the heat alongside those who needed them most. I wasn't sure how many companies and brands would be left when the bad actors finished their hatchet job against decades of equity work and against the Constitution itself. But I determined that whether there were five hundred or five, I would patronize them. I would support them. I would stand on my values.

Ultimately, there are people who seek to build up and people who aim to take down. At any moment, both are loitering—looking for ideas and people and companies to point their energy toward. What this means for all of us practically is there is no guaranteed way to benefit from the former and avoid the latter because their views are often diametrically opposed. This is why it's more important than ever to stand on your values and move with your beliefs. Your values anchor you. Your beliefs guide your choices and investments.

Of course, the need to be anchored and guided through change is not reserved for issues of equality. Human beings resist change in general, and behind each act of resistance is a messy concoction of fear, entitlement, misguided or misaligned purposes, and a dose of self-righteousness. We can't get in everyone's head, and even if we could, the noise would be deafening. Sometimes the best way forward is to reset in what has always been and will always be true—the parts of your life, your company, and your family that are sources and not symptoms. Going back to your values and recommitting to your beliefs gives people something to connect to when uncertainty reigns. It provides a common cause.

In fact, some companies that appeared to be withdrawing from the work associated with fairness and inclusion weren't withdrawing at all. They were mitigating business risk and going back to their roots, working feverishly to redesign processes to ensure that every branch and every flower could survive. They were creating mechanisms to help leaders behave according to their values and to give every employee something to believe in. Worthy goals, but not easily attained. A challenging conversation with a C-suite coaching client made this tension very plain for me.

DESPERATELY SEEKING HUMANITY

When the chief people officer of a storied financial services company reached out to me, she said one of their C-suite leaders needed…help. Apparently this executive had been at the center of a couple uncomfortable interpersonal conflicts. Nothing egregious, per se, but he'd shown a real lack of consideration for others, with little sense of how much his positional power magnified the impact. She wanted me to work with him to support a more inclusive work environment.

I said I was happy to help and scheduled a video call with him for a few days later. I did my homework and had my opening questions all set, ready to observe his responses, take down his words, and clue into the ways he might be open to learning.

The video call quickly turned into one of the most triggering conversations I've ever had—and all I'd asked was "Tell me what diversity and inclusion mean to you."

I'd barely gotten the words out when he launched into it. He wanted me to know how averse he was to "wokeism," Black Lives Matter, and cancel culture (even though he couldn't clearly define the terms). He ranted about "this trans stuff," "pronouns—he/she/they/*whatever*," and went on to suggest that the "war on gender" would be the end of civilization as we know it. He said he understood that racism *was* real and that Black people weren't treated well in the past, but he believed that now it was white men of a certain age who were under attack. He made gross generalizations and accusations, threw his hands up a few times, rolled his eyes, and shrugged his shoulders repeatedly.

When my client finished his diatribe, I wanted nothing more than to click that little door icon on the bottom right of the screen in order to leave. The things he had to say—and the passionate energy that accompanied what he said—knocked me off my emotional center. To be honest, if I weren't contractually obligated to finish out the call, I doubt I would've engaged with him any further.

But I had a job to do, so I forced myself to calm my protective instincts. I made the conscious choice to see him as a human being, one with defining beliefs, emotions, and needs, even if I couldn't quite understand them. As I did this, I realized there had to be something deeper behind all this anger. But what? I shifted into investigator mode, which helps me create just enough emotional space between myself and whomever or whatever is opposite me. I began asking more questions. And I learned a few things.

According to him, he'd once been known as a trusted advocate who opened doors for people—all kinds of people. He saw himself and claimed others saw him as someone who was genuine, accessible, and motivational. Now he felt he had to walk on eggshells—that he couldn't be himself and lead from intuition.

What's more, he told me, there were young people in his life— close loved ones—who accused him of being oblivious to his privilege and blind to the injustices of the world. To them, people like him were the problem with society.

At this point, he got emotional. He felt those he loved most in the world had lost respect for him. This made him feel hurt and misunderstood, and it fueled his resentment toward the ideas and concepts he felt gave way to this perception: *Wokeism. Cancel culture. Black Lives Matter.*

Now, the protective part of me—the insulted part—was tempted to disregard his feelings and invite him to get some real problems. But the compassionate part of me knew his resentment was rooted in the pain of rejection and even scorn. He felt out of sync with the people he cared about. And he hated it.

I didn't get him to change his views, but by quieting my protective mind just long enough to get past his aggression, I was able to ask him thoughtful questions and see the humanity in him. It's tempting to dismiss his kind of posture as simply ignorant, bigoted, self-centered, or even hateful. But many times, it's cognitive dissonance—the psychological discomfort that occurs when certain ideas contradict our beliefs. The higher the discomfort, the more likely a person is to reject an idea. It's as if their psychological survival relies on its dismissal or destruction.

Beneath all the bravado of this client was a genuine fear that legitimizing another's right to exist freely would someday delegitimize his own. It may sound unreasonable, but I think he—in his own mind—was fighting for his life. What he couldn't see was that he'd created enemies where there were none. That someone else's freedom was not tied to his imprisonment. That the battle was in his mind. No one had brought dehumanization to his doorstep, but because he was operating from protection, he was—unconsciously—bringing it to the doorsteps of others, including me and mine.

I think we cling so fiercely to binary thinking because our very sense of self hinges on it. Binary thinking says: *If I'm right and we disagree, then you must be wrong. If I'm intelligent and you don't think like me, then you must be unintelligent. If I'm attractive and we don't have similar attributes, then you must be unattractive. If I'm healthy and your habits are not like mine, then you must be unhealthy.*

Sometimes thoughtful questions give a person a chance to think independently and to be creative. It gives them, and us, permission to evolve. Thoughtful questions don't always work in the moment. Occasionally, people reflect later. Sometimes they come back and want to continue the conversation.

Not every interpersonal challenge will carry such inherent tension. I share this example not because we should knowingly subject ourselves to vitriol, but because it reminds us that when people resist change, when they balk at broadening their lenses, or when they push back on progress, there are often reasons for their behavior that have nothing to do with us or even their stated nemeses. I engage in these discussions not because they're enjoyable—they're not—but because being an effective change leader requires understanding why people resist change and identifying the human need behind the resistance. I've personally resisted change before, and not always because I didn't like what was coming. Sometimes I was just afraid of what I might have to let go.

This is why I love the familiar adage *"Wherever you go, there you are."*

Even if we empathize with people's feelings and can understand the source of their ire, we must be clear about the behaviors we will and will not tolerate. After all, if you punch me in the face, I don't care if it's because I remind you of someone who punched you in yours. I care that I have a black eye.

Clear values, identified behaviors, and accountability are all keys to establishing and maintaining environments where people can do great work together. When you find yourself in a place where others are unwilling or unable to hold healthy boundaries for your benefit, it is in your best interest to make plans to leave or to immediately exit. You have a right to safety, peace, and respect. *You are before the world*, and that includes the world of work.

By the way, the executive I spoke to was encouraged to retire several months after our coaching call. He had no intention of changing and was unable to bridge the gap. Turns out, lashing people with your hurt feelings isn't a good long-term career strategy.

CREATING A NEW VISION

I've been thinking a lot about where we go from here. Every weekday (and some weekends), I wake up early in the morning and, much to my husband's chagrin, check the news. The year 2025 began unfolding aggressively, and because I work directly with business leaders, I feel the need to stay informed. John advises me to focus on what I can control—to avoid spiraling into what-ifs and worst-case scenarios. Sounds good, except worst-case scenarios are occurring at breakneck speed.

It's not in my head. It's not hysteria. It's not dramatics. It's an unraveling unlike anything I've seen, and it takes concerted effort to shake the dull, sick feeling in my stomach that rises when I see that something will happen, tell people it will happen, they don't listen or don't care, and then it happens. Not a morning dawns without an unthinkable headline. Not an evening sets without me wondering what more I can do. I know this: We must first admit to ourselves that what we have is not what we want. For many of us, there's little good to be found in this mayhem, even if you think you're right. Even if you're convinced everyone else is wrong.

I know I'm not the only one feeling this way. I'm not the only one who struggles to conceptualize the length and width of the bridge between where we are and where we should be but who knows we must traverse it anyway. Even as I type, I'm acutely aware that this bridge—more rope than wood or steel—is our new shared experience. It is swinging in the whipping wind. At worst, we fall into the abyss. At best, there will be nausea.

Like an unwanted gift, weapons of psychological war are being delivered to our proverbial doorsteps, and in rapid rotation: The performative National Guard deployments to Washington, DC, Chicago, Los Angeles, and Memphis. The banning of books that broadened our worldview as children and nurtured our empathy.

The replacement of Black History courses in public schools and universities with one-sided, whitewashed, male-supremacist "civics." Each bigoted word and act—each manipulated law, malicious mandate, and twisted narrative—pokes the sleeping bear in each of us. We gird ourselves to give the ire we've been given, and the blast radius blankets more ground than we intend. The larger the area we draw, the more visible the danger. The more visible, the easier to avoid.

We've come to reject the complexity of life and living, opting instead for rigid lines—purely defined categories of things and people. To make sure we don't step on the lines, we back way up from the boundaries we set or that are set for us. Then we watch, waiting impatiently for clear signs of potential risk or reward.

Is this why we're capitulating in advance? Have we adopted the blast radius as a way of life? Have we learned to back way up from the line to keep ourselves safe from ridicule, from responsibility, or from both? I believe this makes our world smaller. It makes us smaller too.

Standing still or going back on this swaying bridge is not an option. The first steps away from our starting point are too brittle now, and the planks on which we currently stand are wearing thin. The unraveling is real, but I've come here to remind you of something that I hope—deep inside—you already know: *We do not have to become it.*

Love and truth are not mutually exclusive. Faith and action must coexist. I believe we are here on the cusp of our own undoing, in part because we've relinquished our right to nuance. Nothing is that pure. We have each been right and wrong. We have each done things we're proud of and things we wish we could undo. No one is all righteous or all evil, and we must ask ourselves how believing this about ourselves or each other serves humanity. I've been humbled as of late. I'm releasing my need to feel important—to be smarter or better than anyone else. I am being liberated spiritually, and the process is inspiring me to do what I can, how I can. And to resist the temptation to try to be everything to everyone.

I don't know what this means to you, if anything, but it's not a call to let those who intentionally wield harm off the hook or to sit idly by while they do. It is, however, a call for greater curiosity—an invitation to pause long enough to discover that which we think we already know. We don't have to embody the very hostility that grieves us.

In early February 2025, when this book was mostly written but I knew there was something more—and different—to say, I felt a spiritual shift. Over the course of many weeks, I stumbled into conversations with people from all walks of life who felt it too. Before these moments of kinship, it was like watching a movie I didn't like but couldn't turn off. Afterward, the image zoomed out, and I could see myself watching the movie. I noticed the marionette strings as I observed my emotional reaction to every post, every article, and every dark report. I found myself thinking about what it would mean to cut those strings—to know bad things were happening but not be jerked around by them—and instead to harness the vision and creativity that had always been available to me and to shape both into something edifying.

You Are Before the World as a restoration story became a finger pointing in my face because systemic failure was everywhere. At the highest level, laws, programs, policies, and practices—things we'd long took for granted—were being consumed by flames. And what I know about fire is that it acts as a catalyst to cleanse and regenerate. I know that after the burning, new life emerges. As it was with my divorce, I couldn't see the promise while holding so tightly to the pain. But when I released my grip, the tension began to ease. Sometimes things must fall apart. And as hard as it was to watch, I wanted to know what was fighting to be born now—and the role I should play in the laboring.

Spirit always finds me when I'm earnestly seeking. During this period, I discovered a few videos of faith leaders, including Richard Rohr, Franciscan priest and founder of the Center for Action and Contemplation, lamenting how organized religion had spoiled God's intent—that Christ is in every person and in everything and that our narrow application of godliness had led us astray. This resonated so deeply. It sickened me to watch people denigrate others, withhold mercy, amass resources, collect guns, and exclude their fellow human beings from abundance. And to do it in God's name was beyond the pale.

It reminded me of when I first attended an evangelical church in Kansas City with a friend. At about the thirty-minute mark, the pastor began condemning specific people and groups, attempting to soften the disdain with the same tired "hate the sin, not the sinner" qualifier. I stood up and walked out—not to be precious but because my spirit was writhing. I could feel my soul rejecting the premise that some of God's children were above others—more important, more worthy, more loved, more protected, or more blessed. I just didn't believe that. I still don't. I knew then that either I deeply misunderstood God's intent or others did, and only time would reveal which was true.

During that period in early 2025, I traveled to the nation's capital to work with a client. The driver who picked me up from the airport expressed dismay at how the city had changed.

"I used to see people walking on the sidewalks, laughing and smiling, having a good time," he relayed. "Now everyone looks sad."

"I bet," I replied, nodding sympathetically. I didn't want to get into a political discussion. I was already spending considerable energy managing my own emotional state.

The next morning, my colleague and I walked the icy sidewalks to our client's office to kick off a two-day leadership experience, and I opened the session by asking how everyone was feeling compared to our first session, which had been many months prior.

"I'm feeling good about our organization but bad about the world," said one of the thirty executives responsible for leading this cherished nonprofit into the future. We were in month twelve of a fifteen-month culture project, and while it had been a long and challenging journey, we were beginning to see the light.

My empathy didn't need help being activated. I walked into the building sensitized to the weight that a purpose-driven beacon in a decomposing city on a hill must be carrying, and I'd wondered if the dichotomy she so eloquently presented was the best we could hope for. It's hard to imagine why anyone would actively work against meeting children's basic needs, but the headwinds were intensifying for this organization and for all of us who work in helping professions.

Over the next two days, we aligned on their preferred future. This included explicating their existing values so employees would recognize them in choices, behaviors, and decisions; ratifying four new leadership principles that made room for every person in the company to lead from where they are; and tightening up governance and accountability measures to ensure that what they intend to create can be sustained. At the end of day two, we invited everyone in the room to plot themselves on a change curve, then asked if they were willing to share the rationale for their placement.

One leader declared that she was at commitment, which is the highest point on the curve, because "this [the culture evolution] *has* to work." She recounted a recent conversation with a strategic partner whose ability to serve marginalized communities relies on the very team that filled the room. It struck me, as she was speaking, that this is the entire point. Helping people, loving people, serving people, and supporting people is not the job of the few. It is the higher calling we have heard and long ignored.

The emotion that had been welling up in me since the morning—since many mornings—crested, and as I extended my arms to hug her, I began to weep. She held onto me. And I let her.

At that point, each day felt like a week. Each week, a month. Each month, a year. I'm known for my composure, but there was only so much professionalism I could muster.

That evening, I stayed with my cousin and his soon-to-be wife, Kimberly, who is a shaman and energy worker. We talked at length about God as love...as light...as a seemingly dormant energy in desperate need of resurgence. We were all feeling the pull toward something rawer and more real. Openly talking about it relaxed some of the tightness in my shoulders. Just before I retired for the night, I asked Kimberly if she'd be willing to hold a session with me the following morning.

I woke up incredibly curious and hungry for understanding. Kimberly led me into her meditation room, where she invited me to sit comfortably in a small chair mat against the wall. The room was cozy, and symbols of her faith journey—along with memories of ancestors she and my cousin had loved and lost—lined the perimeter of the room. She handed me an eye mask and grabbed one for herself, explaining that it helped minimize distractions. She then asked me to set an intention for our session, clarifying that I could keep it to myself, which I did. I closed my eyes and asked God to show me what I was supposed to do now. I genuinely didn't know. I asked for revelation. *How should I use my gifts according to their highest good for a time such as this?*

Twenty-five minutes later, when the session had come to a natural close, Kimberly instructed me to remove my mask. "How do you feel?" she asked.

"I feel fine," I said, meaning I didn't feel any different. That was the truth.

And then she said, "Let me tell you what I saw."

I didn't know that "seeing" was part of the experience, but I sat up straight and took a deep breath.

"You were standing in the middle of a forest," she began. "There were tall trees all around you, and I could see through your eyes. You were looking up to the sky, feeling overwhelmed, verging on panic. And you were so frustrated because you didn't know how to get out. Then an eagle came into view, swooped down, and picked you up. As it ascended, you and the eagle became one"—she put her two palms together with her fingers spread apart—"and you soared to the heavens." Her eyes followed her hands toward the ceiling and her smile was like the sun.

"You are an eagle, Tara. A visionary," she declared with all the hope I needed but had struggled to stir. "You see the big picture and the tiniest details all at once. This helps you know the next best thing to do."

I felt so seen—and carried, like God met me in that very spot in Kimberly's meditation room and lifted me. She couldn't have known I'd written a poem titled "I Am an Eagle" thirty years before. Or that while in the thick of my divorce, my mother prayed for God's protection and dreamt of an eagle with huge wings wrapped around me—silver, white, and cream—just before she woke up feeling assured that I would be okay. And she had no idea that just six days before we sat in that cozy room with masks and chair mats, I'd posted a new *You Are Before the World* newsletter with a quote graphic of Isaiah 40:31 (HCSB):

> Those who trust in the LORD
> will renew their strength;
> they will soar on wings like eagles;
> they will run and not grow weary,
> they will walk and not faint.

In this newsletter graphic, layered behind the Bible verse, was an image of a dense, lush, green forest with an open sky and three birds hovering.

Admittedly, I'm a pattern seeker. It's a trait that has helped me see around corners my entire career and informed both quantum leaps and purposeful pauses. I believe it's this "bird's-eye view" that sets me apart in the leadership and culture space. I'm not smarter or better than anyone else, but I can often sense what's coming and how people and relationships might be impacted by it. At times, this has translated into more relevant, innovative, and useful ideas and solutions. But seeing what's coming isn't the most fulfilling part of the work for me. *It's seeing what can be.*

I thought about my innovation days at Hallmark, during which we learned about a concept called *green-box inputs*. These were bits of insight and various factors that entities must consider as they innovate. The green box usually includes things like strategy, economic realities, consumer shifts, and general trends. In this case, what was unfolding around fairness and inclusion could be considered a trend—a major disruption of the status quo. In the context of innovation, major disruptions don't mean certain death. They do, however, require greater clarity about your competencies, a deep understanding of consumer needs and preferences, a realistic picture of your competitive set, and a willingness to challenge long-held beliefs and norms. If this were an innovation problem, we would gather intelligence, reaffirm our strengths, and set our old playbook to the side so that whatever might come next wouldn't be burdened by it. Disruption invites creativity and courage, transformational thinking, and a return to timeless truths upon which to build timely solutions. Looking at America's real-time deconstruction this way made me feel hopeful.

For entities that really cared about *all people*, the change in

It's Time to Look Deeper

our political landscape and in our society would require a new vision that truly embedded fairness—that ensured visibility, respect, value, and protection for all of us at all times and in all situations.

As many people—especially young people—had been shouting, this couldn't be a *lesser than* or *different from* exercise. We were too broken—too divided—for iteration. This is why people say crisis is the best time for artists to go to work. The opposite of death isn't life. It's creation.

The fact that years prior I'd designed a human-centered starting point for workplace transformation that became The Waymakers Change Group's leading methodology was a God thing. Our methodology was informed by research and didn't rely on acronyms or shorthand. I didn't know we'd end up here. I did, however, know that biological tenets persist through every societal change: *Healthy ecosystems thrive on diversity. We need active participation of all living things for any ecosystem to work. When you mend the deepest wound, you heal the body.*

I couldn't stop thinking about the many brilliant and committed people I know who've worked tirelessly to ensure that everyone in their companies can contribute fully, freely, and fairly. They were having to reimagine the future in a matter of days. Deconstruction is painful, especially when it's unwarranted and malicious. What was happening was akin to arson. I was gutted. But the most strategic among them knew that this deconstruction gave them two choices: stare and rage at the rubble or create anew. In this creation, they were doing what they'd always wanted to do: redesigning systems with fairness at the center and requiring values-based behaviors so all people could support business outcomes and be rewarded fairly.

The answer wasn't easy, but the questions were simple: *Who did we want to be now? Which values did we want to live by? What kind of experience did we want to enable? What did we want to be true about us in the future that wasn't true today?* These were questions only our generative selves—not our fearful or wounded or resentful selves—could answer. We needed to call those parts of us forth now.

While listening to one of Oprah's *Super Soul Sunday* episodes, I heard Michael Beckwith say, "Pain pushes until the vision pulls," and then, "You cannot have what you're unwilling to become." The pain had pushed. The vision was pulling. But I hadn't yet asked myself what I was willing to become. Pursuing the answer is making me feel powerful in the way that rivers are—methodically chiseling paths through rock and dirt, carrying us downstream to a new identity rooted in the kind of human experience we all long for and that we all deserve.

PART II

ARE

Take Care of Yourself First

Dear Reader,
   Have you ever watched yourself wither?
   Lost yourself in someone else's story?
   Made a promise you didn't want to keep?
   Pretended you were okay when you weren't?
   Thought you healed a wound that tore open when you least expected it?
   Been surprised by the universe?

   This part's for you.

Chapter 3

HOW DO I CHOOSE MYSELF?

SOMETIMES ALL YOU CAN DO IS HOLD ON

I WAS EIGHT MONTHS PREGNANT with my third child when I realized my first marriage was over, but it took another two years to say it out loud.

It was the middle of the day, and I'd just waddled into the office I shared with my then husband—a corner bedroom on the second floor of a house we'd built together. Shifting uncomfortably in a worn pleather chair that badly needed replacing, I began searching on a shared desktop for a digital photo of our children for a school project. Almost immediately, I came across a file folder with a title I didn't recognize. Without thinking, I clicked on it. *What am I looking at?* I couldn't tell. The thumbnails were so small. I clicked again. Colors, shapes, and sounds began to form in my brain, and I audibly gasped for air. I remember feeling unbearably hot.

Inside the folder were the kinds of photos and videos no wife should ever see. I must have sat frozen in silence for at least fifteen minutes. My body went limp, but my mind spun in every possible direction. I began reflecting on the weeks and months before. The trips my ex-husband had taken with "friends," the late nights he spent in the office and in the basement "working," and the meaningful conversations we'd had, hoping to salvage what little regard for each other we had left.

When did this start? How did it start? I held my protruding belly and thought about the baby I was carrying. *What was I bringing this child into? What about the two already here?* I'd never felt this many emotions so intensely at once: rage, fear, disbelief, confusion, sadness, and shame.

I began rummaging through piles of paper on the desk for accompanying signs of betrayal, and as is often true, I found exactly what I was looking for. A phone bill—the only bill he insisted on paying—revealed hours upon hours of late-night and early-morning calls and texts. Every evening, when he left our marital bed for what I believed was a burst of creative energy that wouldn't be contained, he went to the basement to call the number staring back at me. I dialed it, and just like in the movies, the melodic voice on the other end refused to answer any of my questions.

"Hi. This is Tara," I said. "I suspect you know who I am."

I could hear her breathing.

"How long have you and my husband been in a relationship?" I asked. It was my work voice, like professional me had stepped in to take over for personal me, who'd clearly fainted.

"Tara, you need to talk to him about this," she said, before hanging up the phone. Hearing her speak my name added insult to injury. To me, it confirmed that I was an ancillary character in a story they shared together. She didn't know me, but she knew *of me*. I was livid. And panicked. And heartbroken. And completely at a loss for what to do next.

My other two children were five and three, and my third would be arriving in a matter of weeks. I was an executive leading an organization of hundreds of people. I was also the primary breadwinner. I loved my husband, but our relationship hadn't been healthy in years. It seemed I, whose corporate career was flourishing, had become a walking, talking symbol of everything he despised: corporate greed, classism, the politics of race, and colorism. I often felt he hated me, though he never said that—until later.

I didn't leave right away. Like mothers all over the world, I felt I owed it to my children to try to save my marriage. The next couple years were difficult as we fought—in the only ways we knew how—to save our family. We had moments of true connection when we thought we might survive the brokenness. But we also had moments of extreme tension that revealed just how different we'd become—me, a rising corporate star with aspirations of even greater leadership impact, and him, a renaissance-worthy artist with uncanny intellect and a rebelliousness to match. Ultimately, it would be a trip to Jamaica that sealed our fate.

One of my best friends, Brenda, stopped by the day before our departure to wish us a good trip and handed me *The Seven Spiritual Laws of Success* by Deepak Chopra. I thanked her, closed the door, and went upstairs to finish packing. My parents had arrived to stay with our children so we could get away—an annual routine we'd only recently instituted to help us reconnect.

The trip started off fine. The resort was beautiful. The weather was perfect. I was anxious but hopeful. We went to the beach, ate good food, watched a few movies. A couple days in, though, I noticed what we were *not* doing: connecting. Between us was a quiet chasm thick with apathy. I kept trying to create meaningful moments by asking thought-provoking questions or planning out our days. He didn't resist, but he didn't enthusiastically participate either.

This is when I reached the chapter in the book titled "The Law of Least Effort." The law of least effort, according to Chopra, is based on the observation that everything in nature functions with effortless ease and follows the principle of least resistance. Each chapter closed with a practice exercise, and this one challenged the reader to stop forcing any action and notice what happens naturally. On this day, I was extremely frustrated because I'd been doing most, if not all, of the coordinating. While lounging on the beach, I attempted to share the load.

"Do you mind getting lunch for us today?" I asked casually.

"I can do that," he said.

Oh, okay. I thought. *This is working already. Maybe it just feels like he's not participating because I'm not leaving room for him to participate!* I felt like the read was already paying off.

Noon passed. One o'clock came and went. By two o'clock, I was hungry. I looked over at him listening to music on his beach lounger and sat up in my chair. And then, as nonjudgmentally as possible I said, "When I ask you to get lunch, and you say yes, but three hours go by and you've not yet done it, what's going through your mind? Literally, what are your thoughts?" I genuinely wanted to know.

He responded, "I'm thinking that when I get hungry, I'll get us food, and if you get hungry before me, you'll get it yourself." I felt shocked but shouldn't have. This one sentence perfectly captured the past few years of our marriage.

The remaining days of the trip went just like that. When I stopped trying, it became evident that there was no trying happening at all. On the flight home from Jamaica, I decided I would file for divorce. Not because of lunch but because whatever we'd once had was long gone. We were both miserable. In fact, as I mentioned earlier, I believed he hated me. He reserved his most antagonistic energy for me and showed zero consideration for my safety, my comfort, my happiness, or my needs. Our children, who were close to both of us, were living their young lives in a void of lovelessness, and no pretending or staying for the children would save us.

The next several months were the darkest of my life. The disdain he felt for me was escalated by my decision to codify what was already there—a broken union. In the separation period, he attempted to tarnish my reputation, break me financially, remove my support systems, and malign me to our children. He called me names, taunted me, and never missed an opportunity to inconvenience me—from emptying the bank account used to pay our bills to squeezing me out of my garage spot during an ice storm. It was hell.

I'd been trying to be a good person through all this, much to the chagrin of friends and family who thought I should match my ex-husband's energy. But I believe we're held to account for how we treat people, including those who don't treat us well. This belief had me obsessed with finding healthy ways to navigate my intense and often conflicting emotions. I was caught in a stranglehold of blame and resentment, both toward my ex and toward myself. In my high vibration moments, I reminded myself that *hurt people hurt people* and that his treatment of me was misdirected childhood trauma. In my low moments, I wished him away, and then I felt guilty for doing so. During this time, I was hardly ever alone, but I was often lonely. While trudging through the shadows, I searched desperately—every single day—for the light.

At work, I leaned in even more. I'd been at Hallmark since I was twenty years old—first as an intern, then in my first official role as a greeting-card writer. By the time my divorce was in process, I was leading the creative writing and editorial department.

Each professional challenge called upon the things I still felt sure about: my curiosity, my compassion, my communication skills, and my creativity. The work and the amazing people I worked with served as healing inspiration. Every day, I got to think about, plan for, and enable genuine connections between people. This was the place where love, humor, hope, forgiveness, and joy came alive in art form and where I was reminded of the endless possibilities available to us when we choose to care and be cared for. My job was proof that these possibilities remained available to me too—bruises and all. Ultimately, it was my job to not only *see* the light but to *create* it and to help others do the same, a salve during an undeniably painful chapter in my personal life.

At home, I found the strength to gather the pieces of me I refused to lose. I allowed loved ones to offer what I needed: refuge, childcare, meals, fun, laughter, encouragement, and kind correction. I learned lessons that helped me live on my terms, like how to embrace self-care, the importance of showing people who you are instead of telling them, and why what other people think about me—especially from a distance—is none of my business.

I hung on by creating routines for myself that guided me through the days. I ate the same breakfast every morning—hard-boiled eggs and turkey bacon—and listened to the same playlist while washing my face and brushing my teeth. India Arie's "Psalm 23" was a constant companion.

I wrote poetry every single night—a return to my earliest form of creative expression. I took my children to the petting zoo and farm every weekend I could. I met with my closest sister-friends, and one brother-friend, for happy hour at least once a week. I began working out regularly and went for walks with my babies when the weather was nice. I consumed spiritual audiobooks on my way to and from work. Every one of these newly formed habits was an act of survival—a rebellious bid to cling to myself.

Through each moment of confusion and grief and fear, I never felt abandoned by God. I did, on occasion, feel far away. Once, at the zoo, Abram stood plastered to the plexiglass barrier between us and a young tiger. He called to him: "Come here, Tiger! Come here!" But the tiger just stared. "I'm right here, Tiger!" he said. The tiger lay still, surveying his surroundings, and blinked slowly. After what felt like an eternity, he rose on all fours and arched his back, lifting his hindquarters, reaching forward with his front paws, spreading his toes. He then sauntered to our little section of the viewing area and touched his nose to the divider. My son erupted in a fit of giggles.

This was me. Standing. Calling. Waiting. Believing God would get to me eventually. Having no idea what would happen when He did. Wishing someone would tell me what to expect.

Through the Fire

Around this time, the obstetrician who delivered my three children recommended I read *The Shack* by William P. Young. The book is ultimately about forgiveness—releasing blame, shame, hurt, rage, hatred, and hopelessness and letting God's love free you, even amid great despair. The read started slowly for me, but my doctor said I'd know when I got to the part that mattered.

One evening, while reading *The Shack* before bed, I got to the part that mattered. The protagonist's journey begins with a heinous act against his young daughter, moves in and through his resulting trauma and family crises, and culminates with a clarion call to forgive. There was no question about what I was being prompted to do. First I thought the words silently. Then I whispered. Then I raised my voice a little. And finally I shouted—"I forgive you!"—and cried for an hour. That was June 9, 2009.

Three days later, I received an email from my attorney

notifying me that the judge had signed my divorce petition. When I opened the document, the date stamp read June 9, 2009. This was just one of many moments that would cement my faith.

I breathed a sigh of relief when the divorce was final, but the roller coaster wasn't over. A few years before, I'd signed for and guaranteed multiple property loans to help my ex build a real estate rental business. I hadn't wanted to take on so much debt, but after hearing "You don't support my dreams" one too many times, I'd surrendered.

One day, the doorbell rang. My ex-husband stood on the porch with a packet of papers in his hand and a vacant smile on his face.

"I filed for bankruptcy," he announced, handing me the packet. "The business is yours now. If you have any questions, call this number," he instructed, pointing to a name I didn't recognize on the top of the first page. "Oh, and I'm leaving town." He turned on his heels and walked away.

I knew I should have asked more questions, but I was in shock. I wanted to scream. *What the hell?* I didn't know the first thing about running a real estate rental business. The agreement had been to sell the properties and pay off the banks. Instead, he threw his hands up and dropped an almost one-million-dollar problem in my lap.

I managed the situation as best I could while trying to figure out a long-term solution, but I was in over my head and the math wasn't mathing. The remaining tenants stopped paying their rent, and the holding banks came looking for me all at once. At the peak, I received between three and five calls per day from each of the four banks. In what ranks toward the top of my most embarrassing moments, a process server showed up at my job.

Picture this: I now owed way more money than I had. I was mothering three young children. My babysitter, who picked up my babies after school and helped with homework, quit without

How Do I Choose Myself?

notice in what I later discovered was an act of self-preservation due to rising—and strategic—hostility in my household. I had a ton of responsibility at work. And while my amazing sister-friends showed up for me when and how they could, my family was hundreds of miles away. *Zero out of five stars.*

To make matters worse, I watched my pristine credit go up in flames (and spent the next seven years rebuilding it). Though I made good money, I spent months in the red, robbing Peter to pay Paul, praying I wouldn't lose my house and my mind. I had to ask my employer for a loan and my mother for money she didn't have. In the end, I settled the debt by writing a check for almost $80,000. (Another God thing I'll get into later.)

Once the fire was out, life began to normalize. I could finally step onto what would be a long and winding road to healing. I looked incessantly for the bright spots, and I found them in both mundane and profound places: a porch chair, a ladybug landing on my finger, sunshine on snow, my toddler's impressive enunciation skills, my eldest child's gluttonous reading habits, my middle child's beautifully aggressive hugs. God refused to let me lose touch—literally.

In the years leading up to this period, I'd often wondered what I was made of. While I thought myself kind and fair, I never felt especially strong, brave, or resilient. I'd always been an anxious person, nervous about everything from disappointing people to suffering bodily harm to failing to meet my own sometimes unrealistic standards. But I survived the worst thing I'd ever been through. And I was beginning to experience joy again.

The following decade brought a period of extraordinary restoration. My ability to see the light generated more light. It seemed that God stood in agreement with me—through a series of minor and major miracles—and ushered in my boldest hopes. Among them, remarriage to my now husband, and with that, three additional children. I resigned from a company I loved to create a company I loved even more. I wrote books and taught courses about leadership and culture and fairness and shared humanity. There were bigger accomplishments, greater joys, and a growing freedom that would find us in the years that followed. It was, and is, a beautiful life.

NAVIGATING A NEW SEASON OF DARKNESS

And then, on that crisp, sunny Texas morning in late 2024, the darkness returned.

As a workplace equity strategist and inclusive leadership expert, I've invested enormous amounts of time, creativity, and energy into cultivating business environments where all people can contribute fully, freely, and fairly. Making a way for all people to thrive is, in no uncertain terms, my life's work. The results of the 2024 US election and the days immediately following revealed an America I knew existed but didn't care to accept. I believed the most marginalized among us would be harmed in ways I couldn't yet fathom. I felt heartbroken. Scared. Rudderless.

On the surface, my divorce and the results of the election have little in common. The former was an extremely intimate war waged in silence that affected very few. The latter, a public declaration with global consequences that would echo across media, classrooms, households, and boardrooms for generations to come. The circumstances could not have been more objectively different, but my emotional response was the same. I felt undone. In both situations, all was given, then rejected, and I was left with the unwelcome confirmation that Black women were still clearing paths we weren't free to walk. Both events severely challenged my values, my beliefs, and the feasibility of fulfilling my purpose.

I had to displace the heaviness in my chest with something I could believe in—something that would protect my peace, my identity, and my ability to make a difference in the world. This numbness, and my unwillingness to go gently into that (not so) good night, gave birth to the book you're holding now.

The journey *You Are Before the World* carried me through in 2025 was no doubt a healing exercise for me personally. The more outrageous things got, the clearer the spiritual call for more light all around us—and not just the profound and earth-shattering kind. The streams, the glimmers, the rays, the reflections, the sparkles—they all matter, and these small glimpses of hope gave me exactly what I needed to take one more step. Climb one more hill. Fight one more battle. Forgive one more mistake.

Sometimes the best we can do is stay in the fight, even if that means retreating to our corners for a bit. I'm always grateful when people acknowledge that continuing is a conscious act of survival. We don't honor the strength it takes to keep going—to believe that hard things won't be hard always. To trudge through mud and brush and wind and rain. To choose to break through when once-sturdy things break down around you. If you're reading this while hanging on to live, love, and give another day, I salute you. It's a necessary start.

KNOWING WHEN IT'S TIME TO LET GO

"I feel sorry for you," he said, straight-faced—in a tone more admonishing than empathetic—while leaning forward in one of the chairs that framed the corner of the bedroom we once shared. It struck me that, in the almost seven years we'd lived there, this was the first time we sat like this.

"Do you?" I replied flatly. Whether I asked or not, he was poised to explain why. I didn't invite him over for his sympathy. I invited him to declare that our months-long separation was about to become a full-fledged divorce.

"Why is that?" I looked directly into his eyes. *Show no fear.*

"I feel sorry for you because no good man will want to be with you."

This is what we're doing now? I swallowed hard and forced an "Oh" that sounded like a question but wasn't.

"You'll be a single, middle-aged woman with three young children," he continued. Then...*wait for it*..."And you don't know how to submit."

A violent stream of insults rushed to the tip of my tongue, but I bit them back. *First, I didn't know it was my job to submit. Second, I would willingly follow a leader going somewhere worthwhile.* Instead of using my outside voice for an inside conversation, I uttered a not-at-all sincere, sarcasm-ladened, "Thanks for your concern."

I wanted him to leave. Until this day, he'd been (mostly) cordial and even loving at times. In the space between that fateful trip to Jamaica and this raggedy attempt to break me down, there'd been flowers. Good conversation. A couple high-effort outings. And campaigning. He'd expressed a strong desire to stay married and made countless promises about the many things he would never do again.

I'd considered it. For our three young children, of course, and because—like millions of women all over the world who've experienced this unraveling—I didn't get married to get divorced. I'm not a "grass is greener" person. And I didn't expect marriage to be easy. In fact, I'd not grown up in an "easy marriage" household. I remember asking my childhood best friend, Keri, if her parents fought in private, because I never saw them speak an unkind word to each other and I figured maybe it was because I was there.

GETTING OFF THE CROSS

Throughout my childhood, my father battled alcoholism. When he drank, he was volatile—loud, angry, confrontational, and unpredictable. His drug of choice made him easily triggered at home and on the road. I can still see my six-year-old self, cowering in the backseat of his yellow Volkswagen Bug while he played automotive Frogger at unimaginable speeds—forcing cars to the side of the road, exiting to approach the target of his ire, threatening to yank people from their seats. This was such a regular occurrence that I dreaded riding with him. In the worst moments of his disease, he would rail against my mother and she would shrink, doing her best to calm the stormy seas she knew too well while trying to keep his alcohol-induced tirade from spilling over onto me and my brother.

Her mother—my grandmother—wasn't a fan of my father. He was an activist in the 1970s stateside fight for Cape Verde's African independence. He was also a bit of a ladies' man and had more machismo than his five-foot-five frame might signal. But he chose Mom, and she chose him. In the months before Nana's death, she came to appreciate the best things about him—his humor, his knowledge, his results orientation, his fearlessness, and his willingness to jump in and fix any and every broken thing. He was a problem solver and showed up for people in ways that made him hard to forget.

I never outright asked Mom what it felt like to be in a clearly complicated relationship. On a random weekday when I was about fifteen years old, I had my first run-in with her suppressed rage. Dad had been ranting about something I've since forgotten. When he left the house, I ran into my room and slammed the door, and within minutes she rushed in—fists flying. I lay face down on my bed and covered my head with my hands. She was crying uncontrollably.

"Don't you ever disrespect me like that again!" she wailed. The sound of her pain cut like a knife.

I was confused. She'd never laid hands on me in a way that wasn't gentle and kind, but here we were. My confusion quickly turned to empathy. Her outsized reaction to my immature action wasn't about me. She was tired, angry, and raw. That day, the verbal aggression she'd long endured overcame her. Oddly, I remember feeling useful when the fist-full windmill ended. She was my best friend. I just wanted her to feel better.

My father was, and still is, a paradox. Living with him during the good times taught me I could do anything and be anyone. That the sky was the limit. That no one was inherently smarter or more capable than me. He made me and others laugh easily with his razor-sharp wit and tall tales. He was the best storyteller, and though we never knew how much of his stories were true, it almost didn't matter. Dad was larger than life in all the ways young daughters need their fathers to be. He was strong, smart, and an able protector. While small in stature, no one challenged him because he was known to physically bite anyone, anywhere. He fought dirty, which I assume was a subconscious response to being chronically underestimated. Overall, his glow was much larger than he would ever be. Unfortunately, so was his shadow.

Living with Dad during the bad times taught me how to conceal my true emotions, walk on eggshells, people please, and pretend. A happy father meant a peaceful household. It meant that he would tell amazing stories. That my mother wouldn't get yelled at. That my six-foot-two brother wouldn't be made to feel small. These are lessons I never wanted to learn, and decades later, I found myself practicing them regularly in my own marriage. Mom never wanted me to follow in her footsteps in this way. I didn't want that either. And I certainly didn't want it for my own children.

My decision to file for divorce after months of separation was prompted by two very specific experiences. The first came while watching a Sunday sermon on television about how people get stuck in bad situations. "God will guide you right out of a bad situation and into a more promising future," the preacher said.

"But because the bad situation is familiar, you'll turn around and walk back into it. You'll romanticize the past by saying things like, 'It wasn't that bad,' or 'Maybe it will change.' Do not go back—God moved you for a reason."

When the preacher spoke those last few words, I looked uncomfortably around the room, half-expecting God Himself to magically appear and point a finger at me. After all, in my unhappy union, at least I knew what to expect, what to avoid, and how to steel myself for periodic bursts of anger or disillusionment. It wasn't fun, but it was familiar. And when you're faced with an uncertain future, sometimes that's enough. The preacher's words convicted me. I felt exposed.

HONORING THE GOD WINKS

The second experience happened at a local movie theater. I'd gone solo to see *Nights in Rodanthe*, a story about a woman who seeks refuge from a painful divorce at a friend's oceanfront bed and breakfast. A male guest who's going through his own darkness journey comes to stay the weekend and—through power outages and bouts of relational intensity—they fall head over heels in love.

He departs, and over the next several months, they exchange detailed letters about work, life, and their love for each other. They plan a highly anticipated visit to her home, but he doesn't show. Naturally, she panics. Weeks later, his son arrives on her doorstep with a box of mementos in hand. Her great love had died in a tragic accident.

The protagonist slips into a deep depression. For weeks, she's inconsolable and hardly leaves her bed. Her teenage daughter—who'd blamed her for the divorce—steps in to help with daily tasks, including caring for her little brother. One morning, the woman walks outside to the porch swing, where she sits and stares listlessly into space. A few minutes later, her daughter steps into her view and says softly, "Tell me about him."

After a moment of silence, her mother responds, "You know, there's a kind of love that makes you believe anything is possible." She then turns to her daughter and says, "I want you to know that you can have that."

This line pierced my heart like an arrow, and I was instantly reduced to tears. My daughter Kas was eight years old at the time, and I realized that if I didn't make a change, I'd be teaching her what my good-hearted mother inadvertently taught me: that walking on eggshells is a reasonable sacrifice. That you must contort yourself into a version of you your spouse feels comforted by. That silence, sacrifice, and suffering are the prices you pay for partnership. I left the movie theater determined to go through with the divorce. I'd already done the hard part by overcoming my inertia. Now I just had to keep putting one foot in front of the other.

I think it's important that we don't ignore the seemingly small moments that call to us—that remind us we are part of a shared human experience. Maybe it's a perfectly timed phrase spoken by a character who is fighting for something you also want for yourself, maybe not. But there are moments of witness that hold lessons we most need when we most need them—a reason you watched that movie, found that article, or are reading this book. It's okay to let it move you.

Chapter 4

SAY GOODBYE TO SELF-SABOTAGE

You Can't Keep Being the Good Person

While the decision to end my marriage was the ultimate letting-go experience, the most difficult chains to break were mired in my mind. I had to surrender control because I didn't know what would happen in the months and years to come. I had to release the shame I felt for failing to keep the most important commitment I'd made to date. I had to quiet the notion that motherhood required being with your children all the time, instead of the fifty-fifty custody arrangement divorce sometimes necessitates.

And hardest of all, I had to give up my deep need to be seen as a "good person." Some of the best people I knew had stayed in bad marriages. They'd endured. *Wouldn't a good person have figured out how to keep loving someone if they promised they would? Wouldn't a good person simply absorb their partner's pain and keep walking the high road?* Turned out, in my case, it didn't matter how high the road was. It took seconds to travel from it to rock bottom.

There were early indicators that my ex might go scorched earth on me. He was angered by my decision to leave the marriage but also hurt by it, and I know when things don't go our way or when we're afraid, we look for someone to blame. I sensed I would be that person for him. I was right.

Navigating the scorched-earth era of my divorce was a mind-bending trip. Generally, I had a reputation for being a good person. Fairness is one of my core values, and this means I sometimes wait too long to make tough calls or to hold people accountable for their actions. The excuses I make for others' bad behavior spin through my mind like a methodical and never-ending Ferris wheel: *Maybe they can't help it? Do they know they have options? They must not have the tools they need to do this differently. This is probably a trauma response. Maybe I just need to work harder, communicate more, be more patient, ask more questions, give it more time, be more supportive.*

There are few people on earth who can find more ways around an interpersonal mulberry bush than I. While in the thick of the divorce, my friend Kim Carter said something I've never forgotten and have repeated to countless people since. We were enjoying a meal at a local restaurant in Kansas City, and I shared some of the unfortunate experiences I was having. She listened intently and asked a few pointed questions. Then the velvet hammer: "Tara, you have the gift of mercy, and sometimes you overuse it."

Damn! I remember how deeply understood I felt. In one sentence, Kim affirmed the light in me while illuminating the shadow on its underside. Her insight helped me process, then embrace what it means to be a balanced human being—both kind and truthful, giving and discerning, loving but not limitlessly so.

Growing up, I always aimed to be easy to love. If I were easy, my father would make us all laugh. If I were easy, my mother's life would be more peaceful. If I were easy, I would make more friends. If I were easy, my teachers would give me good marks on my report card. I was conditioned to go with other people's flows, even if that meant silencing my voice and ignoring my own needs.

I got good at mirroring people's goodness back to them, and I looked for myself in their judgments of me. Most of us have some degree of childhood trauma. For me, being easy to love was a trauma response to growing up with a volatile parent. I learned from Dr. Alduan Tartt, a friend and Christian psychologist based in Atlanta, that I was fawning.

Fawning is a term coined by psychotherapist Pete Walker. It describes a trauma response that we adopt to avoid conflict and establish safety, and it develops from experiences related to complex PTSD or from being in situations of interpersonal violence.

In researching fawning, I discovered there are seven primary behaviors:

- **People-pleasing:** Doing things for others to gain their approval or to make them like you
- **Suppressing emotions:** Denying your true feelings for fear they may not be honored or understood
- **Difficulty setting boundaries:** Having trouble establishing personal boundaries to protect yourself or your values
- **Prioritizing others:** Putting the needs of others before your own to preserve relationships
- **Having trouble saying no:** Struggling to say no, even when saying yes compromises you in some way
- **Agreeing with others:** Agreeing with others' preferences to the exclusion of your own

- **Holding yourself responsible:** Holding yourself responsible for other people's behaviors

The list read like a manual for my life. In talking with Dr. Tartt, I realized how misunderstood people-pleasing behaviors are. We talk about it as a personality trait, using phrases like "She's a people pleaser" as a slur meaning "She's weak minded." But anyone who's experienced trauma in any form knows it's much more complicated. People-pleasing is how we keep the peace, how we avoid magnifying discomfort, and manage the perceived fragility of our attachments.

For me, breaking the chains of childhood and adult trauma would take years of effort. I still have moments when I need reminding, but the transition from easy wife to independent woman marked the beginning of cutting to the front of my own lifeline—of putting myself before other people's needs and expectations, before their assessments and perceptions. *Me before the world.* It was when I first started asking the question "What will happen if people get mad at me?" And accepting the truth in the answer: "You will not die."

We pretend we don't care about these things. That we are above them. Sometimes we lie. If you admit it to no one else, admit to yourself that more than once, you have cared too much about what people who have no real impact on your life think of you. You can't stop doing something you don't cop to.

TAKE UP ALL THE SPACE

At least once a week during my writing process, I wondered if anyone would care. That's what I'm wondering now. Our stories are familiar to us, and we take familiar things for granted. Reading about your own evolution in black type on a white page doesn't feel especially engaging. I calm my inner critic by remembering that my favorite stories are favorites because they make me feel validated as a person and because I learn something while reading them. I discovered a different way to see myself, to understand my experience, and to translate seemingly benign moments into momentum.

While most who know me think they know me well, few do. I'm a thinker. A tinkerer. A doodler. A ruminator. I'm private. Protective. Skeptical. At times critical. Sensitive. Curious. Giving. Loyal. Hopeful. I'm an encourager. A teacher. A helper.

What I am not—not anymore—is dispensable.

In some ways, the stories I've told so far feel unimportant in a book about helping. At the same time, they represent what I want most for you to know. Because I almost disappeared.

The day the words "I want a divorce" left my lips, it was on the heels of a troubling visualization. I saw myself as a towering figure holding on to something tiny between my thumb and index finger. The tiny thing was billowing, like delicate fabric—silken threads separating from their form with each gust of wind. I stood there, transfixed in seeming nothingness. As the scene closed in, I could see that the billowing thing was not a thing at all. It was me, flailing—two legs and one arm waving in panic, the other arm in its keeper's grip. *I was holding on to myself. By a thread.* And I knew in my spirit that if I didn't leave the relationship, I would disappear. I would lose myself. Maybe—quite possibly, quite likely—forever.

I'd been shrinking for years. In my first marriage, early wins were shared. Poetry performances. Awards. New jobs. Raises. A first home the color of sunshine. A baby with a perfect little face.

As the years passed, my ex-husband's artistry expanded, always more layered and complex. But the career opportunities didn't manifest the way he wanted and probably deserved. I tried to be encouraging, following his emotional arc: hope, disappointment, hope, frustration, hope, righteous indignation, hope, anger, hope, disillusionment. It was hard to watch someone so unquestionably gifted not get his due. And it was especially hard to grasp his professional reality alongside my own, which was flourishing.

I'd worked on products featuring Iyanla Vanzant, Bishop T. D. Jakes, and Chris Rock. I was promoted multiple times. Once, I got three raises in two years. And I was working with Dr. Maya Angelou on a series of product offerings. (This was a working relationship that outlasted the marriage.) These experiences were a source of great pride for me, but the contrast between our trajectories was stark, and it seemed his frustration was spilling out and over.

He stopped being excited for me. Stopped being proud of me. Stopped showing interest in me. So I stopped sharing my accomplishments. I didn't think he cared to hear them, and I believed he saw me as a symbol of a system intent on holding him down.

This feeling was solidified during a counseling session. When I discovered the infidelity, we agreed to work on our marriage. The psychologist was a slight Black woman who was known for being kind, wise, and direct. He'd begun seeing her separately, but during our first joint session, she told me I was "suffering from white privilege." At the time, I was confounded. Years later, I would come to better understand how certain physical traits of mine advantage me in a society that favors whiteness, but I certainly didn't think I was wielding those traits as a weapon against my own husband. In counseling, we never got to the infidelity part or the imbalance in household contribution or the financial issues or the anger or the lack of consideration. My light skin was apparently the force behind every transgression. I felt scapegoated.

I had no idea how to fix any of this, so in true fawning fashion, I made myself small. I spoke softly. Walked gingerly. Laughed less. I looked for any opportunity to celebrate him, hoping to even the invisible scales. I shrunk not because he asked me to but because I was afraid not doing so would put a nail in a coffin that appeared to have our last name scrawled across the top. Looking into the eyes of three innocent children, this didn't feel like an option.

I thought about this years later when a friend shared that his first wife pretended to be someone she was not. He said she acted like she liked what he liked and enjoyed doing what he enjoyed doing. He said she pretended to be okay with things she was not okay with. As he explained this dynamic, I immediately envisioned Vanessa Bell Calloway's character in *Coming to America* standing on one foot and barking like a dog. My friend's wife projected flexibility, patience, tolerance, and boundarylessness. She was, I thought to myself as he painted the picture for me, an easy wife.

But life isn't easy, and when you're trying to build a home with conflicting blueprints, the foundation will shift and the walls will buckle. Personally, I didn't believe she was pretending. I believed she was trying to be who she thought he wanted. Because she wanted him.

We do this all the time. We contort ourselves to fill the spaces offered to us because we want the love or attention or reward the space provides. And when in the natural course of living we grow beyond its parameters, we do one of two things: we constrain our potential by hiding our light or we break the box and lose things—jobs, friends, spouses, or identities.

In the end, making myself small did not keep my marriage alive. It merely postponed the inevitable. I knew that if I married again, it would have to be to a man who loved me when I stood up straight.

TENDING TO YOUR WOUNDS

If you're still with me, you may be thinking this is a book about divorce. If you've been through a divorce or are going through one now, you may want it to be. You are likely finding your own experiences on each page, tucked into mine, like Easter eggs but without the resurrection. It reminds me of a Hallmark term called *universal specificity*, where we'd use language and ideas that felt especially relevant to the recipient of a card but that were simultaneously relevant to millions more.

I've been on the receiving end of countless calls from women who are considering, going through, or healing from divorce. They don't want advice. What they seek is assurance that they will survive—that they'll come out the other side whole and happy, because they see wholeness and happiness in me. But while my restoration story begins with the most broken I've ever been, *You Are Before the World* is not about brokenness. It's a love story, and in it, I am the lover and the beloved.

Emerging as a stronger, healthier version of myself after childhood trauma and grown-up heartache didn't happen automatically. It was not a "time heals all wounds" situation. I did not just figure it out eventually. There was no checklist, planner, or agenda that propelled me forward. I fought my way through that forest, picking up tools, shields, maps, and flashlights along the way. Prayer and fortitude were constant companions. I found comfort in the spirit-centered habits that started and ended my days.

Years later, when I'd been restored relationally, professionally, and financially, I finally decided to deal with the lingering wounds of my divorce. My decision was prompted by an exchange with my current husband. We were watching a popular television show, and the main character was embroiled in a torrid affair with a beautiful woman. Throughout the show, I kept loud-whispering snide comments.

"Death to side chicks," I scoffed in random response to seeing her on screen.

"She must hate herself," I diagnosed, denigrating her aloud for willingly playing second fiddle.

"You get what you get," I judged when she cried because he still hadn't left his wife.

My husband looked over at me, confused and disappointed. "Why are you being so mean?" he asked pointedly.

Mean? Me? Did he watch the same show I watched? Wait— was he defending her? To hide the rising tide of tears burning in my throat, I swiftly exited our theater room and shuffled into my office, where I proceeded to fall apart. He followed me and sat on the corner of my desk.

It never fails. You can have decades of life lessons under your belt, people can look to you for insight, wisdom, and inspiration, and still—unhealed wounds tear open unannounced and swallow you like dry ground in an earthquake. One finger pointing at that wound—even when extended from the hand of a person who loves you—is painful and bewildering. I was snotting at this point and filled with an agony I cannot describe in words. My trauma was the very blood running through my veins.

"Tara, look at me," he said.

I didn't want to. I already knew my reaction looked like overreaction, but it was a reflex. I didn't think about, plan, or control it on its way out of my body. It exploded from a part of me where a long, uneven scar still had a tiny slit on one end.

"I know you went through a lot," he said. "But it's been years. When are you going to get help to process this?"

He didn't have to name "this." We both knew what "this" was, because infrequently but too frequently, it popped its rotting head from beneath the foundation of our otherwise beautiful union. He'd been patient because he loved me. He'd been supportive because he felt compassion for me. But the schtick was getting old. It was time for me to stop looking for the infidelity monster under every bed and in every closet.

He suggested I go to therapy. I'd been seeing a therapist for a few years but hadn't peeled the onion to the center of my most challenging thoughts and feelings, the ones potent enough to spoil the best things in my life: my present marriage and the family attached to it. When people who've not been to therapy tell you to go to therapy, they think it's straightforward—that you schedule an appointment, sit on a couch, unpack your pain, get advice, and walk out a conqueror. They don't know how long you spend circling every topic but the one you went to tackle. Many first downs. No points.

My therapist recommended EMDR therapy, which stands for *eye movement desensitization and reprocessing*. It's designed to help people process traumatic memories and lessen the vividness and emotion associated with them. I'm not a therapist, so I won't attempt to tell you how it works, just that it *did* work. The experience revealed something profound for me: what I believed was a simple betrayal wound was much deeper. There were issues of unworthiness so ingrained in me I no longer recognized them as separate from myself. The betrayal only reinforced an inferiority complex that preceded it—a consuming fire that raged in me whenever I feared being bested.

In the EMDR process, my brain returned to old memories. *"Move the plant, little boy," the firefighter instructed from the fire escape outside. I ignored him at first. There were no boys around. Just me, staring through the closed window of the small, second-story apartment my parents shared. "Move the plant, little boy," he called again. "I'm not a boy," I replied, with all the emphasis my shyness would allow.* He was trying to rescue me from the room my great-aunt Tetea got locked out of when I closed the door behind her. She was afraid. He was frustrated. And I was trying to make this man understand that he was rendering me invisible. I was two years old. This is my first memory.

I was not like any child I knew. I was well-loved by my family but not well understood. With a curly, uneven Afro and hand-me-down tees and shorts, I was often mistaken for a boy. "He's so cute," people would gush as they greeted my mother. She'd kindly correct them, and I would bury my face in her skirt. I spent most of my early years looking for corners to write in and papers to draw on. I inhaled fantasy films where impossible things became possible. I devoured books in which shy protagonists solved riddles others missed because they were too busy being the hero. It was in my own mind—where I regularly got lost until I found myself—that I made sense of a world that seemed wildly disinterested in me.

Not only did I look like a boy, but I was also objectively funny looking—an especially unfortunate thing for a person whose mother had been a beauty pageant queen in my small, insular Cape Verdean community. My father was as handsome as she was beautiful, with unmatched charm.

And then Duane barked at me on the bus during a fourth-grade field trip. One of the girls traipsed to the front, where he sat among a small crowd of boys, to tell him I had a crush on him. He swiveled his head over his shoulder to look at me, barked like a dog, and let loose a hearty laugh that rapidly became a chorus of hollers and knee slaps. In one of my EMDR sessions, I identified this as the moment I learned I was ugly. The following decades held considerable evidence to the contrary, but the wound remained and made me painfully insecure and deeply afraid of public ridicule.

It's hard to imagine that after years of loving and being loved, a woman can keep pressing play on a forty-year-old diss track, but it happens. It happened to me. Through therapy, I was able to reconcile old ideas and emotions that had plagued me. The entire journey unlocked a deeper level of empathy for my inner child and for those who hurt me, including my ex-husband. I don't believe he was out to get me. I believe he was experiencing his own reconstruction process, that it was messy, and that the demolition dust got on my shoulders and in my eyes.

The realization that low self-worth undergirded my pain opened the door to so many questions. Is this latent feeling of unworthiness why we tolerate mistreatment? Is it why we beg people to love us, even when we are, in fact, the prize? Is it why we don't ask for what we really want or why we say yes when we mean no? Is it why we laugh at jokes we don't find funny or get caught in emotional spin cycles when we fear someone doesn't like us—whether we know them personally or not? Is this why we draft social media content twenty times before we post it? Then check it five seconds after, to see who liked it or commented or shared it—then press delete if no one engages with it—so others won't know we're invisible?

And why do we think that time will magically heal these hurts? Why do we hesitate to seek help when we clearly need it—when our life choices and experiences keep reflecting our pain back to us? What would it mean to not only feel worthy but to know that we are? And, perhaps most important, would we help differently if we didn't believe that our help was the reason people love us? If we weren't afraid that pulling back might get us uninvited to the places we most want to be?

Uncovering a self-worth wound resets the playing field and changes the game. There's not a winner or a loser. You are your own opponent. My sense of wholeness was, at least in part, facilitated by EMDR therapy. But staying whole has meant accepting that tending to wounds is a lifetime commitment.

Chapter 5

RESTORATION

You Have to Accept What Is

"HERE'S WHAT I WILL say," announced my cousin Matt, right before another of his relatable comments about how nothing is as it seems and everything is as it seems: hopeful and hard.

He, my brother, Jon, and I were on a video call, exchanging aging parent sagas.

Matt is a mediator, which is evident in his speech, tone, and approach to all things people oriented. He was updating us on his mother—my father's twin sister—who was forgetting things she used to know. Getting confused. Repeating herself. Becoming easily frustrated. He'd just lost his father months before and was still holding considerable grief. It seeped out while he was responding to an unrelated question, but when you're grieving, everything is related. Grief doesn't wait for an invitation or a lull in conversation. It interrupts like a hungry toddler—needy and now. Matt shared that he'd been super edgy.

Jon had been dealing with these behaviors for years—not within himself, but with a loved one who lives with him and his family. Life was getting harder at his house for everyone. He was exhausted from the daily grind. He was also trying to save other family members who needed help but wanted it in ways that would hurt them even more. His health, which he'd worked hard to improve the year before, was declining again.

"That's a lot," I affirmed. "How are you seeking support?"

"Nobody gives a shit," Jon snickered. But Matt and I knew there was nothing funny about it. Like our father, Jon folded his most challenging emotions into jokes. It's easier to be funny than to be frail.

"People just want me to be strong," he said. "To fix broken things and make calls. To cook and show up at events. To be steady. That's all they care about. That's what I'm here for."

I'd never seen my brother look so beat. I was in the middle of writing this book at the time, and while I wrote it to help women put themselves before the world, it occurred to me that we are not the only ones who need help. Women pour everything out, but my brother and cousin were stacking everything up on their shoulders—and it was clearly weighing them down. We scheduled a monthly call so we could support each other through a ride we knew would get more tumultuous in the months ahead.

We knew the ride would get more tumultuous because my aunt is not the only one showing signs of memory loss. My and Jon's father—born the second youngest of six children by a matter of minutes—has dementia. His oldest sister died of Alzheimer's disease, as did his second oldest sister. The next sibling is in cognitive decline. There is only one of the six whose memory remains intact. And as children of this once-vibrant sibling set, this truth weighs heavily on us.

If you've ever loved a person with dementia, you know that reality is subjective and immediate. It's the person looking back at you, the food they're eating, the clothes they're wearing, or the way they're feeling. It's the memories they still have—whether from yesterday or twenty years ago—in the current moment you're experiencing together. Dementia leaves no room for context or clarifications. I don't argue with my father about whether he really got into a fight with the neighbor last week. I know he's remembering a fight from thirty years ago and that it feels like it happened last week.

This happened fast. My husband, John, and I moved my parents from New Bedford to a three-bedroom house around the corner from us after two concerning incidents: a cancer diagnosis and a near-fatal heart event. My father arrived on a plane from his birthplace with my mother and a brand-new pacemaker. Mentally, he was as sharp as ever. However, in three years' time, after a few more (though less severe) heart events, it was evident he had changed.

There have been both agonizing and hilarious moments along this journey. Agonizing is watching him behave impatiently with my great-nieces and great-nephews. Hilarious is the conviction with which he recounts his experiences—and as his disease progresses, makes up new ones. At my great-nephew's birthday party a couple years ago, my father wore an arm brace. A partygoer's mother, concerned, asked him what happened.

"I pulled someone out of a burning car," my then seventy-eight-year-old father said with a straight face. I shot my niece a look, and we covered our mouths to suppress our laughter. My nephew, her husband, walked by and shook his head. I glanced at my mother, searching her eyes for answers. She looked away, pretending all was normal. She was getting good at that.

The inquirer stood there with her mouth ajar. Just in time, one of the children ran by and tripped on the patio's edge, providing a welcome distraction. (She was fine.)

It took a few weeks for me to realize my father hadn't fibbed that day, though tall tales were core to his identity. He was remembering a real experience he had while working as an emergency medical technician decades before. In that job, he saw things no person should see. He saved people from cars, buildings, and their own poor choices. Some—including a nephew who died in his arms—he couldn't save. I would never fully appreciate how these moments of tragedy and near tragedy must have affected him. I do know he was always preoccupied with danger. He still is.

Somebody I Used to Know, a hauntingly beautiful memoir by Wendy Mitchell about her journey with early onset dementia, helped me better understand the disease. "You might think about the memory of someone with dementia as a mass-produced bookcase," she wrote. "The bookcase is full of books that contain factual memories." She goes on to explain that our oldest memories are on the bottom. Our most recent, on top. And if someone shakes the not-so-sturdy shelf from side to side, the ones on top fall off first.

This is what was happening to my father. Early on, when we could still talk about his memory loss rationally, before the impairment became severe and he lost insight into his own condition, he'd drawn a line in the sand: "If the day comes when I can't remember you, I don't want to be here."

I chuckled to put air back into the room. "Is that right?" I said in turn.

"That's right. If I can't remember my baby, put me out of my misery." He was laughing but dead serious. My father is a straight shooter who often uses humor to soften the blow. When his cardiologist told him to stop eating pork rinds, he complained that he didn't want a life without pork rinds: "If pork rinds are gonna kill me, I guess I'll be dead!"

If my mother is the light of his life, I'm the apple of his eye. Right now, it brings me peace to know that this disease is not personal—that it will take things from him, my mother, and the rest of us that we don't want to lose. I've considered how I'll feel when my father stops recognizing me, and while I've embraced this possibility from the beginning, I've given myself permission to be devastated when consideration becomes experience.

The most important lesson I've learned about loving my father in this state—when he is not himself and yet exactly himself— is to not argue with his reality. In any given moment, his truth is all there is, and how I respond directly affects the moment after. Because his brain is accessing the only reality he remembers, being corrected is incredibly disorienting for him. I try to imagine someone telling me every day that what I know is true is not true. I'd be perpetually frustrated.

I've trained myself to nod my head and offer a well-timed "Really?" or "Is that right?" Then "What happened next?" or "Say more about that?" My aim these days is to make him feel heard. But there are extremely challenging moments, when the worst behavior he's ever demonstrated pulls forward and I feel eight years old all over again.

One of my favorite quotes by Angela Davis says, "I am no longer accepting the things I cannot change. I am changing the things I cannot accept." There's a lot happening right now that I don't like, and I believe in fighting good fights. I also believe there are many forms of self-preservation. One is to stop fighting unwinnable wars.

"Accepting what is" is not giving up. It's a refusal to squander our energy—a decision to stop resisting the wrong things so we have enough fuel for the right things. The deterioration in my father's brain is an unwinnable war. It's too advanced to treat, so we're focused on care, safety, and my mother's sanity. The fight for my brain is a different story.

I found out after completing a nutrition genome test to learn more about my food tolerances that I have a double dose of APOE, known as the Alzheimer's gene, which puts me in the highest risk category. I can't change this fact, but there are things I *can* do to support my brain health. I can ask the neurologist how to mitigate my risk of premature memory loss, and I did. I can stop drinking alcohol, and I have. I can eat more superfoods, and I do. I can do cardio for thirty minutes a day, and I've started working out again. I can drastically reduce my sugar intake, which is a struggle, I won't lie. But I'm doing it. And in a choice to care for my heart—and to relieve myself of undue stress and futile frustration—I can love my perfectly imperfect father. I can forgive him for his mistakes and celebrate him for the many ways he is and has always been magical. I can listen as he tells his stories again, and I can laugh like it's the first time. I can honor his survival story, his accomplishments, his best efforts to love us and protect us and make us proud. I can honor his humanity. And I will.

Get Clear About What Matters

While editing this book, I've had many crises of conviction. My family and close friends know how protective I am of my personal life. My go-to line is, "If people want to tell my business, they'll have to make it up." I give no fodder. No details. Few photos. You'll not find a chronicle of my second act on social media—just snapshots. I give only what I can afford to have interpreted, which isn't much.

But I was prompted to tell my restoration story. Writing this book has been an act of obedience, and I pray you get from it what God intends. I don't know what that is for you. I do believe that for helpers, the personal part matters. We find ourselves overwhelmed not only by the societal loads we carry, but also because of suffering that might exist in other parts of our lives—because work isn't working or the partner isn't partnering. Because parents need parenting or parenting won't quit. Scratching and surviving at home while serving in the streets is a recipe for disaster. I was a disaster. And restoration means little if you don't appreciate the destruction that preceded it.

Life after divorce rivals any rebuilding process: you demolish things, you evaluate the rubble—deciding what to keep and what to toss—and you work to put the pieces of your life back together in a more durable form. You forget what you knew before you had to survive a hostile environment. It's not about rebounding but about bounding forward in a whole new way.

One rarely discussed divorce hazard? Dating myopia. I made this condition up, but if you've ever seen just a narrow slice of what's true about someone, you can understand it. Picture this: Your ex never complimented you. You meet a new person. They compliment you without ceasing. *You are the most beautiful human being who ever walked the earth. Your hair is fabulous. Your smile is like the sun. You smell like heaven.* You overvalue this trait in them because it's the same shape of a hole you've been living with for too long, and it feels good to not notice the void. Unfortunately, you fail to pay attention to anything else—like how they don't keep their word or how they expect you to make all the effort or that you've not met anyone important in their life. Red flags, all. But you can't see them. You're too busy admiring the plug in the hole.

This happened to me when I started dating, which sounds benign until you kiss frogs you thought were princes, reinforcing the most profoundly disorienting unintended consequence of divorce: an erosion of trust in your own discernment. *I didn't see it coming. Why didn't I see it coming? What else will I not see coming? I saw it and ignored it. Why did I ignore it? What else will I ignore?*

I admonished myself for marrying someone who turned out to be so far from what I needed, especially since some disconnects were evident when I accepted the proposal. My first marriage yielded three incredible children. I could never regret it. It's also true that it wasn't a good fit. I guarantee he feels the same.

One post-divorce evening when the children were with their father, I called a college friend for dating advice. He listened to me drone on for a bit, then cut to the chase.

"Do you want to get married again?" he asked.

"Someday," I said wistfully. "I'd like to reestablish family for myself and my children. It's my greatest hope."

I was anxious about whether and how this might happen, but I wanted to be honest about what mattered.

"Try writing a letter to God asking for what you want in a husband. And be very specific," he added.

My brow furrowed, and my mouth curled to one side. I wasn't sure how writing a letter would bring me a husband, but I figured there was some manifestation stuff going on that I didn't fully appreciate. At the very least, I admitted the writing exercise was intriguing and might teach me something.

"Okay," I said. "Then what?" If there were Jumanji-like instructions to this trick, I needed clarity.

"Just do it," he said. "Keep me posted."

My first draft looked good. I wrote down substantive qualities like humor, responsibility, character, and honesty. I added chemistry, communication, and some other attributes I thought would yield a good result.

The following month, I met a man online who mirrored my list. We spent quality time together, but two things went horribly wrong. He was impatient with my children (a nonstarter), and he was carrying substantial baggage from his first marriage. I suppose we both were, but his baggage was always in the foyer. He frequently told stories about his ex-wife, often related current observations to past debacles, and got visibly shaken when I'd say something that reminded him of her. After celebrating a holiday together, he broke things off.

My feelings were hurt, but in true Virgo fashion, I immediately went back to my letter to make corrections. Clearly, I missed something! I noted that I'd written, "God, please send me a *man* who . . ." I deleted that line and replaced it with "God, please send me a *husband* who . . ." Specificity. I then added a phrase about seeing my children as a gift, not a burden. I wanted someone who was willing to guide and shape them. I put a fine point on the letter and tucked it away.

Later that year, I pinged an old college bandmate on Facebook. (Yes, I was fishing.) He didn't respond—at least, not right away. We weren't close in school, but marching band members spend a lot of time together, so we'd been friendly. I was on the dance line representing Spelman, and he was in the drumline at Morehouse. Back then, I paid him little attention and he paid me none.

After two weeks, he reached back, and we began a conversation that revealed a staggering depth of alignment. His marriage had recently met its end. We each had three children of similar ages. (He said he'd always wanted six children.) We had parallel career trajectories. We liked the same foods. We enjoyed the same travel destinations. We valued the same things, had complementary goals, and held like beliefs about faith and family.

In those early days, I didn't get much done. We talked on the phone each night for hours about everything and nothing. I felt like a schoolgirl again, except with children, bills, and a very big job.

He told me he was scheduled to be in my city for a business meeting and asked if we could hang out, floating that he might stay the weekend. I responded that dinner would be nice, not wanting to put too much pressure on either of us. The next day, he called.

"What city do you live in again? Kansas City or St. Louis?"

I tried not to laugh. These two cities are four hours apart. *How do you have a meeting in my city if you don't know where my city is?* I was tickled by the scheme and flattered that he put so much creativity into seeing me.

Most telling during this discovery period was his intentionality. It obliterated every excuse I'd made for men who failed to keep their promises and reinforced conventional wisdom from older, wiser women: *Men will do what they want to do.* I wasn't the least bit confused about his interest. There were no guessing games.

Just before he boarded his plane, he said a thing that made my heart soar and my stomach sink: "If our connection in person is anything like it's been on the phone, it's a wrap."

It's a wrap. It is complete. This is it. You are the one.

My heart soared because I felt the same way. My stomach sank because the *if* meant we were in limbo. I felt chosen, and I wanted to keep feeling that way.

I picked John up Friday evening after I left work, when his "meeting" was over. He was nothing like the life-of-the-party, twenty-year-old bandmate I remembered. He was calm, measured, and confident. Solid. Easy. We drove to Jazz, a Creole restaurant in Kansas City with amazing pasta and better vibes. After a circuitous conversation about dreams, goals, and plans, he smiled knowingly and looked into my eyes. Then he paused to make sure I was listening.

"What?" I asked. There was chapter and verse in his head. I could see the wheels turning.

"It's a wrap," he declared. "I'm done." He sat very still, holding my gaze.

I tried to talk him out of it. Every stupid, thoughtless decision

I'd made since my divorce rushed through my mind like a river, a veritable flow of foolishness.

"It's too soon," I said softly. "You need to heal from your own ending. Recovery is difficult." I touched his arm for emphasis. I believed he needed time to make stupid, thoughtless decisions too, and I didn't want to be one of them.

He smiled and shook his head in that way I've come to know so well. "I'm good. I got this. I'm clear." And then, with an outstretched hand, "I need you to take a leap of faith with me."

I swallowed hard. *What would happen to me if I followed this feeling, then fell on my face? How long would it take me to get up? What would I lose on the descent?* I thought about the answer I gave to my friend about wanting to get married again: "It's my highest hope." I knew great reward came with great risk—the very point of a leap of faith. This is what mattered.

"Okay," I said. And in a God-ordained instant, I had a spiritual partner.

I would see that same knowing smile a thousand more times in the years to come. It is the look of self-assurance—of someone who doesn't waste a lesson and who meets life with both curiosity and wisdom. It's the look of a man who doesn't borrow trouble, who deals with facts when (and only when) they present themselves, and who solves problems with logic and reason. John is an engineer, and together—with our family—we would construct a love and a life of significance.

This life we share has been punctuated by "God winks"—perfect timing, cleared paths, open doors, and dreams coming true. In our home, we have visible reminders of God's hand on our life together. One of them is the revised letter I wrote about my ideal husband, which sits prominently on my husband's nightstand. In it, I asked God for a husband who would add to my children's lives by sharing his gifts and having fun with them. A husband who makes me laugh. One who would challenge me without being combative. A true partner who is responsible and has integrity. A man who is steadfast.

For helpers, knowing what matters is clarifying and protective. What matters comes first, without exception. If there are sacrifices to be made, what matters is not on that list. For me, family matters. It gives my life purpose and makes everything else worthwhile. This is a lesson I would learn very early in my relationship with John, when I faced a consequential choice between family and career.

Do What Counts

Knowing what mattered led me to my person. It also steered me away from a thriving career. An aspiring writer and artist, I'd wanted to work at Hallmark since I was fourteen years old. I enjoyed twenty-one years engaging with brilliant people who taught me about business, helped refine my creative skills and talents, and encouraged me—then positioned me—to lead. After years of professional achievement, I landed on the succession list for my dream job. When we decided to build a life together, John lived in Texas with his biological children, and I lived in Missouri with mine. My career couldn't continue as planned unless I remained in Kansas City, and that wasn't an option. For reasons centered on the needs of our children, it made more sense for me to move to Texas. *Know what matters so you can do what counts.*

Leaving Hallmark initiated a mourning period for me, but it also laid the groundwork for what came next. While I'd been moving toward that "deluxe apartment in the sky," I did not choose it. I walked away from the possibility of a C-suite job and the additional money and influence that went with it. I chose family. I chose love, restoration, connectedness, and partnership. Soon after I resigned, I found out that the job I'd been prepared for would be available six months later. It stung to learn that after seven years of intentional preparation, I was so close. God knew. I did not. And even this was divine.

John has asked on multiple occasions if I have regrets. The answer is no. While it was indeed a loss, I never questioned whether I did the right thing. Knowing what mattered turned losing a long-held dream into an abundant promise beyond what I could yet see, and it opened the door for me to do what counts.

Knowing what matters and doing what counts catapulted my career to new heights and allowed me to help others: family, friends, colleagues, clients, and communities of people online that I've never met in person but with whom I share a common purpose and bond.

Doing what counts has also served me personally. During a conversation with Dr. Tartt about the imbalance between women and men, he claimed women should ask their husbands to do more.

"Men don't fully appreciate how much work women do," he said, acknowledging the invisible work of women and mothers all over the world. "We get to wake up, work out, go to the job, come home, eat, and do it again the next day. Y'all are running around doing all that, plus everything we don't even notice or appreciate."

He was right, of course. I had friends teetering on the edge of madness, desperately clinging to hope that the next day would be better than the last. That just one of the several all-consuming fires would fizzle out. That some benevolent soul would come along to lighten their load. Every morning, they woke up with this hope. Every night, they went to bed disappointed. I remember those days in my own life as the two-glass days, because for several months during my most difficult stretch, I drank two glasses of wine every night to help me sleep.

"Sexism is a hell of a drug," he said plainly. "It's not right. It's not fair. Women should ask for more. *You* should ask for more."

"Who, *me*?" I asked, seeking clarification.

"Yes, *you*! You should ask for more from your spouse. You deserve to have a balanced partnership."

"I'm good," I replied, laughing awkwardly. I felt a twinge of embarrassment. The truth is, I'm not entirely sure I have a balanced partnership. In fact, it may be true that my husband carries more of the load than I do. He manages the finances. He puts the garbage out. He washes the cars and fills them up with gas without me asking. He feeds the dogs every morning and night, unless he's on the road, then I do it. He prepares our yard for the change in seasons. I used to do laundry, but since he's better at it, he now does it. I manage a couple of the services we use inside the house and plan our travel and family vacations. I facilitate substantial household purchases when needed and freshen the décor now and then. I grocery shop and cook most of the time, and he cleans the kitchen. When I don't feel like cooking, I order out and don't get any lip. We both work full-time jobs.

When our children were young, John helped with math and science, and I was on duty for reading, writing, and history. He coached our kids' sports, and I helped with art projects.

We are partners. We feel equally responsible for the quality of our marriage and the safety and happiness of our family. We've had two major arguments in the almost fifteen years we've been together. The fights are few because we're in alignment, but also because we care more about each other than we do about being right. We can calmly discuss complicated feelings that would send most couples into fits of despair. We put each other first, and our children know this, which is why they never tried to play us against each other. Together, we've become more successful, more prosperous, more content, and wiser over time. We make each other better, and we know it. So, no. I do not have to ask for more. Not this time.

I saw Gary Zukav speak at a conference a few years ago. In

his best-selling book *Seat of the Soul*, he describes spiritual partnership:

> [Two people] are partners on a journey of spiritual growth. They want to make the journey. Their love and trust keep them together. Their intuition guides them. They consult with each other. They are friends. They laugh a lot. They are equals. That is what a spiritual partnership is: a partnership between equals for the purpose of spiritual growth.

This tracks for me and John. Zukav also points out that spiritual partnership isn't always romantic—that we can join hands and hearts with any person intent on spiritual growth and travel with them to a place of greater enlightenment. This is important. Not everyone is coupled. Not everyone wants to be. Still, I believe we're not meant to walk this life alone.

John and I keep each other grounded in what matters and work together to do what counts. We have made, and continue to make, a beautiful life. I joke with John that he is my spiritual reward for longsuffering—for the times I wanted to lose my religion but didn't.

To say God restored my heart and my soul in this union and in every life-altering thing it has brought—including three more children, two grandchildren, and amazing in-laws (including a sister)—would be an understatement. I shudder to think about where and who I'd be without the clarity and courage it took to let go of old things so I could take hold of new ones. My second act, fueled by a more expansive mission, unleashed my helper instinct, revealing fresh ways of making a difference and providing the resources necessary to follow through. Time, along with trial and error, has highlighted both what's most important and what's most effective.

Helpers, you can't do everything. There are only so many

hours in the day. So many days in a week. So many weeks in a year. When we spend our time swimming upstream—or worse, doing the dead-man float—we put undue stress on the one life we've been given. And when we deprioritize our own needs to fulfill the needs of others, we grow resentful.

Dr. Maya Angelou wrote, "A woman in harmony with her spirit is like a river flowing." Finding our flow—and doing that which helps us stay there—is a game changer. Doing what counts is an exercise in discernment, but it's also about drawing harder lines around ourselves and our priorities.

Chapter 6

GETTING FREE

SETTING LIMITS

BEFORE WE MOVED TO Texas, the three children I birthed—Kas, Abram, and Anthony—attended a Kansas City charter school called University Academy. The student population was 82 percent Black, and the teachers and administrators were attentive, caring, and committed to providing a quality education for all. They fostered a strong sense of community and collaborated to educate the children, keep them safe, fuel their imaginations, and support their growth. My three children were happy there, so I didn't take moving them across the country to a predominantly white community and school lightly. But they weren't the only ones in for a shock.

I'd heard stories about the Texas neighborhood we were moving to—that sports were a big deal, that many of the moms stayed at home, that school events were frequent and elaborate. When we first relocated to Texas, I was still working full time for Hallmark and traveling to headquarters in Kansas City every other week.

I'll never forget my first Teacher's Appreciation Week in our North Texas suburb, where five of our six children were spread across elementary and middle school. One fall afternoon, our youngest son, Chase, pulled a piece of folded paper from his Spiderman backpack and handed it to me. It read as follows: "Hi, Parents! Teacher's Appreciation Week is around the corner! Below please find our daily themes!"

At the kids' former school in Kansas City, we had Teacher's Appreciation *Day*. As a busy mother of three, I'd purchase gift cards and call it finished. The memo went on:

- Monday: Gift your kiddo's teacher their favorite flower!
- Tuesday: Give your kiddo's teacher a gift card to their favorite restaurant!
- Wednesday: Gift your kiddo's teacher their favorite snacks!
- Thursday: Write your teacher a handmade thank-you note!
- Friday: Student's choice!

I looked down at Chase, who was staring at me with eager anticipation, then began assessing the situation. "Did you get this note about Teacher's Appreciation Week?" I asked Anthony. He nodded. Then, to Christopher: "Are they doing this at your school too?" Yes. Everyone said yes. They were all buzzing around me as they were beginning their post-school routines: snacks, homework, and more snacks.

I know this sounds nice. I'm not saying it wasn't. Teachers have one of the hardest jobs in the universe, and they deserve to feel appreciated. What I *am* saying, though, is that each of our five school-age children had multiple teachers. An average of three, to be exact. I multiplied five children by five days by three teachers. That was seventy-five gifts! I stared at this note for a few minutes, walked over to my husband, thrust it against his chest, and said flatly, "No."

"No, what?" he asked, confused. (I have a very bad habit of finishing statements out loud that begin in my head.)

"No, I'm not curating seventy-five gifts for Teacher's Appreciation Week. I have a full-time job." I defiantly walked back to my office and plopped into my chair.

My words flowed with conviction, but I felt a pang of guilt. Would my children feel disappointed? Would they be ostracized because I refused to acquiesce to this demand letter? Would their teachers think their mother was selfish and mean? Or worse, not paying attention? It didn't help that John's ex-wife was a creative maven, and I knew she'd make enviable gifts for the teachers of the two boys she birthed. They would look so thoughtful, and so would she. (Side note: this is an accurate depiction.)

Was I not thoughtful? Or maybe I was thoughtful, but with caveats? I didn't have the time or mental fortitude to pour myself into this task. Many of the school moms were on multiple committees where they set up tents at sporting events, ran science fairs, and coordinated school supplies. I was conducting research, leading projects, presenting to customers, and cooking for a small basketball team. I didn't think myself better or worse, but we were not the same.

I asked John, who was also busy managing multiple work priorities, what he thought I should do. We weren't new parents, but we were new at parenting so many children together, and he was more familiar with this suburban world order. In true John fashion, he responded, "I don't care. Do what you want to do."

I asked our children how important it was to them that I go all-in on the list. They shrugged their shoulders, which I took to mean they kind of cared but not too much. In the end, I asked them to choose a favorite teacher, and we complied with three of the days: gift card, flower, and handwritten note. Shady? Perhaps. But a happy medium for them was better than a miserable low for me.

When I gave birth to Kas, my friend and Hallmark colleague John Dill, who has since passed on, taped a tiny piece of paper to my computer. It was a quote by Jill Churchill that read, "There's no way to be a perfect mother and a million ways to be a good one." I would repeat this phrase to myself numerous times while raising our children. I repeated it when there were two games scheduled at the same time and John and I had to divide and conquer. I repeated it when a work trip overlapped with a Fun Run. I repeated it when the book fair ended before my meeting did. And I repeated it when the school solicited moms to help with orientation but I just donated school supplies instead. I chose to believe that my life and work would mean something to my children someday and that my love for them was understood.

I didn't think much of this until our children were older, but I was—and still am—a bit of a "heady" mother. They came to me when they were refining their college essays. They'd ping me when they needed fifty dollars and didn't want their dad to know. They still talk to me for hours about relationship dramas or societal concerns. But I was not the PTA mom, and it wasn't just about the time. My social anxiety creates very real peopling thresholds.

Setting limits on what I could reasonably do helped keep life manageable, but it wasn't the only consideration. Over the years, I've also had to consider *how* I do things and *with whom* I do them. I called my friend Melissa to talk to her about this, because she'd recently set limits of her own while immersed in the fight of her life.

SAY NO TO PEOPLE PLEASING

For context, Melissa is one of the most optimistic people I know. She can find a silver lining on a heap of discarded dreams piled high in the corner of a dank alley at midnight. Hand her your burdens, and she'll return them light as a feather. Tell her your anxieties, and she'll remind you who—and whose—you are. Show her your doubt, and she'll exchange it for belief—the kind that sees reality as a contributing factor, not a determining one.

Melissa is widely known as someone who shows up for everyone and everything, but when she found a lump in her breast that led to a stage 3B, triple-negative breast cancer diagnosis, she turned inward.

"I'm not inherently a 'force to be reckoned with' kind of person," she shared. "Some seem to knock down barriers in a blaze of fury. That's not me. I have to be intentional. I have to stay focused." She offered this as her reason for retreating.

"What helps maintain your focus?" I asked, realizing there'd been few times in our almost-thirty-year friendship that I'd seen her withdraw or withhold anything. She was quite literally a yes person in the most generous way.

"When I *really* want something." Her voice changed. It was deeper. Grittier. And her prominent brown eyes became slivers of moon. I wanted to know what prompted the energy shift. Melissa is usually smiling, even when discussing serious topics. When she stops smiling, for any reason at all, it's arresting.

"Like *what*?" I sounded desperate. I was.

"In the past, it was wanting to be successful at this or that. Wanting to experience something new and knowing that accomplishing a thing meant I had to step up or push through. That I had to make my works match my faith." She paused to take a breath and lifted a tear from her cheek. "Then came breast cancer. And I really wanted *to live*."

The sentence soared with all the gravity you'd expect. This idea isn't foreign to any of us. We've all wanted something badly and found ourselves focusing intensely on every step that might lead to it. But there are categories of wanting. You can want a date or a job or a house or a car. Or you can want to live.

For Melissa, digging into the belief that God would carry her through the cancer journey was her first and most fundamental survival strategy, and it set the stage for the curation that would come. She shifted her perspective toward what mattered—the values she learned at the hip of her mother: *Be good to people. Give what you have. Help how you can. Keep your promises.* All her life, being a helper had set Melissa apart. At the same time, experiences like the one she recounted to me illuminate the many ways we are finite. It struck me that when you're fighting for your life, you can't be too good to people at your own expense. You can't give more than you have. You can't help too much. You can't keep promises to others and break them to yourself.

This realization earned its exclamation point when Melissa told me what happened just before her lumpectomy. She'd agreed to participate in a research trial using a combination of drugs at the teaching hospital that was home to her care team. This meant giving more blood than normal, answering more questions, experiencing more inconveniences. In the moments before the doctor put her to sleep, the research conductor asked permission to take extra tissue samples from her body for their study. After explaining the mechanics to me, she took a deep breath.

"What did you say?" I asked, and relaxed my face, which I could feel was contorted.

"I said no," she responded—with spice.

"And what was going through your mind when you said no?" I volleyed back to her, wondering how her no jibed with the trial she agreed to participate in.

"That cancer had taken too much from me already," she

asserted. "Chemotherapy basically poisons you. Radiation burns you. Now they were about to cut me, and I couldn't agree to one more violation. I couldn't let them treat any part of my body as a lab number. I'm not a specimen."

Melissa's account reminded me of the times I agreed to something, then discovered it wasn't good for me but felt bad about changing my mind. Instead of advocating for myself, I went along because "I put myself" there. This is a familiar scene, especially for helpers. Melissa on the hospital bed. Me in my marriage. Maybe you in a job. It takes courage to say no when people are waiting for compliance and when denial is uncomfortable, inconvenient, or socially unacceptable.

"I was calm on the outside, but inside I was screaming," she added. The words fell from her lips in a whisper, which emphasized her point.

Being more concerned about how others perceive the limits you set than the emotions that necessitate them is not a good feeling. Black women in the world are conditioned to remain calm—to appear unmoved. Resistance is perceived as aggression. Denial is perceived as selfishness. Boundaries are perceived as rejection. We survive environments not built for us by suppressing our emotions. But the emotion goes somewhere. I believe we absorb it—that it causes us physical and psychological pain. We are, from a physiological standpoint, shortening our lifespan every time we swallow our discomfort to avoid disappointing people. I asked Melissa what else, practically speaking, moved her through her cancer journey. How else did she keep herself focused on living?

"I limited my social circle during this time. I couldn't let anything break the concentration required to survive. I didn't want to explain myself to people. I didn't want to be on the receiving end of unsolicited advice or to hear stories about others who had my form of cancer but didn't make it."

I knew she'd done this, but I didn't know it had been an intentional choice.

"Did you feel isolated?" I asked.

"Not really. It wasn't about being alone; it was about having the right circle of people around me. People who would pray for me. Who would meet me in my moment without using my moment to have their own moment."

I wanted to shout when she said that.

She went on. "People who would support me in ways that were truly helpful instead of the ways they thought would be helpful. I knew, because of my personality, that they would want to be supportive. And that I would feel compelled to make that easy for them, even if I didn't want the kind of help they were offering."

I broke out in full body chills. *Is this how people feel when we drop off broccoli casseroles after the death of a loved one?* I let her words land hard on me. She was saying, with crystal clarity, that even when we're not okay, we accept things from people we don't want because it makes *them* feel better. *Lord.*

"People-pleasing wasn't in the cards," Melissa said. "I didn't have the energy for it."

"And how did this limiting process make you feel?" I asked sincerely. "How did you experience it?"

"It was empowering," she said, "to decide how I was going to move through this journey. I needed to be in control of it, and I was."

Melissa's cancer is gone. She still goes for screenings every six months, which serves as a reminder of how strong her body was for her when she needed it to be. In all, she lives with greater awareness, greater intentionality, and greater strength, having found value in setting limits that keep the main thing the main thing.

Like Melissa, I began seeking mindful ways to set limits.

When you have five school-age children and a full-time job, mindfulness is not easy to come by. Every day is like making your way through an amusement park. You're just holding hands in rotation, trying to decide what ride to get on, hoping you don't miss the next ride while waiting on the first. All the while, people are hungry, thirsty, and need to go to the bathroom. In my brief but intentional moments of stillness, I started noticing the resistance in my life—situations and relationships that make me feel tense or that force me to think too hard, plan too long, or work around unnecessary barriers.

Overthinking how to tell the truth because I know someone won't want to hear it? *Resistance*. Spending energy I don't have to overcome someone's unrelated trauma? *Resistance*. Doing work I don't have the skills or credibility to do because others think I should? *Resistance*. Throwing money at an idea when it has no momentum of its own? *Resistance*. Waiting a bad situation out, hoping it will improve if I exercise patience? *Resistance*. I started letting things fall away—and in some instances, removing them, because I know that wrong things don't get right with time.

Helpers struggle with this. We want to show up when we're called. We want to be the person who goes through a storm with those we care about, and even with people we don't know. We want to believe we did all we could to save, bolster, protect, and mitigate. But when we shrink in the shadows of our helping, it breeds resentment. And when the person or situation you sacrifice yourself for doesn't get better? We add the weight of perceived failure atop existing fatigue.

Societal chaos had forced me to get clear about what I'm truly responsible for. My sphere of concern is greater than my sphere of influence, and my sphere of influence is greater than my sphere of control. Now I try my best to focus on what matters and do what counts. What matters is my family and friends, my health, my purpose, and my peace. What counts? The choices I make. The work I do. And how I do it.

STAY OUT OF GROWN FOLKS' BUSINESS

"I'm staying out of grown folks' business." This was John's response the first time I expressed frustration about my father's unwillingness to take his memory medicine.

"John, he needs his medicine," I said, pleading with him to see my side. "If he doesn't take it, he's going to decline faster, and that will put strain on Mom." I hoped he would agree that I should intervene.

"I understand that. But your father is a grown man. Your mother is a grown woman. What are you going to do?"

"I'm going to tell him to take his medicine," I said matter-of-factly. There may have been a baby foot stomp. There was definitely a neck roll. I was indignant.

"You plan to go to their house multiple times a day to force-feed him?"

"Of course not," I replied. Now he was being ridiculous.

"So, I'll ask you again: what are you going to do?"

I hated when he made so much sense. The truth is, beyond encouraging my dad to take his medicine and supporting my mom in her efforts to facilitate that process, what *should* I do? I can't make a grown person whose bills I don't pay do a single thing. Ever.

During a neurology appointment, the nurse practitioner asked Dad if he wanted to complete testing that might clarify whether his vascular dementia is now combined with Alzheimer's. Last time he tried, he'd only gotten through a couple exercises at the top of a very long list.

I took this opportunity to try and wield my Daddy's Girl influence.

"Dad, I do wish you would try again to complete the test," I said gently. "It would be helpful to know if we're dealing with Alzheimer's. It affects more than just you. It affects me and Mom too." I was hoping to draw on his love for us.

He looked straight at me, scrunched up his face, and said, "*You* have a nice day!" Then he struck the floor with his cane and looked away. That was that.

This realization rippled outward for me. If how my parents managed Dad's disease was their business and not mine—meaning not something I *should* or *can* control—then I didn't have to stay awake at night worrying about it. I didn't have to rack my brain trying to solve a problem no one asked me to solve. Or carry a burden of responsibility that was not mine. Or constantly seek information about a situation that wouldn't change my role in it, just so I can be in the know. Wanting to be in the know is a deeply entrenched Virgo trait. I get it honestly, and we tease my mother about this all the time.

"Have you heard anything else about the fires?" Mom asked one time when John and I stopped by to get the mail. "Your nephew is there." The Los Angeles wildfires of early 2025 were still spreading, and she was wringing her hands.

"No, I've not," I replied. "Have you?"

"No. I want to call your brother, but he's dealing with his own troubles. I don't want to bother him."

Using John's strategy, I said, "I'm sure if something were happening with him that you should know about, Todd would call you. If you've not heard anything, I'd assume he's fine, or that he will be." I said this very rationally, knowing that I'm often that person pulling the *what-if* thread until I'm completely unraveled.

"But he was in a hotel, and they were going to move him. I wonder if they moved him. Do you think they'll move him?"

Calm as a cucumber, John wielded his superpower: "There's no way for us to know that, Mom."

"I guess you're right," she said.

When John says "There's no way for us to know," he means we should stop speculating. He means that when we spin through every potential outcome absent facts, we worry for no reason. I changed the subject so Mom could think about something else, at least for a few minutes.

I'm learning the hard way—very hard—that we can be concerned about people's well-being without obsessing over or feeling responsible for their outcomes. We don't have to make someone else's hard thing our hard thing. Now, having six young adult children gives me ample opportunities to test this principle. When you see yourself as a lighthouse—a guiding star in another's dark night—it gets intense. I've never done anything as hard as parenting young adults. No one tells you when the right time is to shift from controlling their environment to influencing their thinking to supporting their decisions to just loving them no matter what they do, which, at some point, becomes none of your business.

This idea of staying out of grown folks' business applies to so many facets of life. It can be the antidote to gossip, misplaced worry, workplace drama, and more. I may be concerned, but I can simply let people know I'm around if they need me and let it be.

It reminds me of the time my friend Jasmine sent a screen shot to our small group chat. Her facialist had broken up with her on Instagram, citing a difference in political opinion and values. Her exact words were, "We are not aligned."

Our immediate response was that Jasmine should keep it moving. Turns out, it wasn't that simple. The woman was more than a facialist; she was a friend. They'd been to each other's homes, shared intimate details of their lives, and known each other for years. She trusted this woman so much that she recommended her to all her friends.

We had a call scheduled later that day, and Sasha, one of the friends in our sister circle—ever gracious—began with, "I want to apologize. I didn't realize this was an actual friend. That does make the situation more complicated."

Does it? I wondered. I find electronic breakups childish. I asked what prompted the message.

"Nothing!" Jasmine responded emphatically. "I hadn't said anything or posted anything recently. She just came at me." She was shaking her head in disbelief. "Who does that?"

"Sounds like a personal problem," I shot back reflexively.

My words didn't come out quite right. I didn't mean Jasmine shouldn't care about the end of the friendship or that it shouldn't hurt. I only meant that it seemed this woman was feeling conflicted within herself and I didn't think there was anything for Jasmine to do. The facialist hadn't opened a door to mutual understanding. She just made a unilateral decision to end the relationship, citing irreconcilable differences, and there was a period on the end of her sentence.

At one time, I would have advised Jasmine to reach out for more information—to ask for a conversation or an opportunity to find common ground. But I've finally learned to use John's superpower and mind my business.

"Other people's business" is anything people think, feel, or experience that doesn't concern me unless they invite me into it. This includes unpleasant feelings or negative beliefs they might have about me. If they don't help me see what they see, which might give us a chance to address it together, it remains their business. To me, this was one of those instances.

It took me a long time to find peace with this approach, but it keeps me out of emotional purgatory. I may sense someone is unhappy with our relationship. Maybe they won't return my calls or they're abrupt when we do talk or they're edgy around me. I used to stay up at night in torment, wondering if I did something wrong. I would spend hours scripting a reconciliation speech in my head. But now, in this new era where I refuse to be undone by foolishness, I won't beg people for their love or understanding. When John says "Sounds like a personal problem," he doesn't mean we shouldn't care. He means not everything is ours to investigate, understand, or fix. This posture has helped me tremendously. I've stopped chasing people. For anything at all. The world is on fire. Who has time for games?

Let Them Use Their Own Brain

When I first heard John share the idea of using one's own brain to one of our children, I cringed. It sounded mean. Our third youngest child, Christopher, otherwise known as the "second middle," had knocked on our door and asked how to fix the chain on a bike he wanted to ride.

Without looking up from his phone, John said, "You have a brain; why are you trying to use mine?"

I'm pretty sure I gasped. Our son stood there for a minute, then turned on his heels and walked out of the room.

"Damn!" I said.

"What?" John clearly saw nothing wrong with his response. "He'll figure it out."

Our son returned a couple times with follow-up questions. If he tried something but it didn't work, John would give him something else to look up, and he'd leave again. After an hour or so, our son walked back into the room, proud as a peacock. He'd figured it out indeed, and with his own brain!

Most of the time, people are perfectly capable of finding solutions to their problems, but we jump in too soon and stay too long, interrupting the natural learning process. John could have told our son how to fix the broken thing. But he wouldn't have learned how to do it himself. He would have been robbed of the newfound confidence displayed proudly on his face.

When we first blended our families, I'd spend an hour in the kitchen every evening before a school day making lunches. It was an insane assembly line. Our oldest wasn't home at the time, so lined up on the counter were five lunchboxes and five categories of food: drinks, fruit, chips, a sweet treat like cookies or fruit snacks, and all the ingredients needed for sandwiches. Each of these piles was a mess, because Abram liked fruit punch and Anthony liked apple juice and Chase liked orange juice and Kas and Christopher's drink preferences changed. The same was true of the chips and fruit and sandwiches, down to meat choice and meat density, bread preferences, and condiments.

John walked into the kitchen one day while I was engineering lunch. "What are you doing?" he asked, with more judgment than interest.

"I'm making the kids' lunches." *Wasn't it obvious?* I was proud of myself—it was a sight.

"They're fully equipped to make their own lunches, you know," he declared without breaking his stride. He then shouted from the other room, "As long as you do it, they won't!"

In a few words, he conveyed two things: I was taking on unnecessary work, and I was giving them a pass. I felt I was showing my children love by making their lunches. Maybe they felt that way too. But it's also true that we can fall into patterns of doing things for others that outlast their usefulness. Especially when those you're helping don't *need* your help.

Helpers take on unnecessary work all the time—other people's pains, fears, needs, hopes, wants, and curiosities. Sometimes we don't even think first; we see a gap and instinctually dive into it, without considering how we hurt ourselves by adding overwhelm to our lives or how we hurt others by enabling them—by depriving them of the discomfort that facilitates growth. When I finally stopped making lunches, I was slightly embarrassed by what a nonfactor it was. I told my children they'd have to make their own lunches from that point forward. I was mentally prepared for mutiny, but their responses were simply, "Okay."

Minding my business doesn't come naturally to me. I was a very nosy child and am a curious and concerned (read: nosy) adult. Embracing this practice has freed valuable space in my brain. Now when issues come up that feel Tara-adjacent but not Tara-centered and my body perks up to respond, I pause and simply ask myself: *Is this my business?* More times than not, the answer is no.

I'm confident there are people out there tapping their fingers and bouncing their knee, waiting for me to intervene, chase them down, or use my brain to fix their problems. Now I let them wait. I'm spending more time shrugging my shoulders and shaking my head.

You Are Enough

When I hear the phrase "You are enough," I think, *Enough of what?* Turning fifty has reconstituted me. I don't want to be enough. I want to be content—with who I am, what I have, and what I aim to accomplish. To me, contentment means feeling satisfied. At peace. Sufficient. It means existing in a perpetual state of gratitude.

Contentment is what my girlfriends and I talked about for hours during a weekend trip to Arizona in the summer of 2024.

"I'm burnt out," Jasmine sighed as she sat on the edge of the pool, her slender brown legs swirling clockwise in the lukewarm water. It was the hottest part of the day, and while August in Arizona isn't ideal, this was the one weekend the three of us were available. A successful entrepreneur, she'd worked fifteen years in an emotionally draining field that requires a saintly level of impulse control. The work alone could lead to burnout, but it was also the hours piled atop self-induced pressure to show up for family, her partner, and her friends in all the ways good children, spouses, and besties are expected to.

We were living and working in an era inundated with talk of burnout. The plethora of books, articles, posts, and movies made it clear that collective exhaustion was taking women by storm. According to Dr. Tartt, by the end of 2024, Black women had begun leveraging the Family Medical Leave Act (FMLA) to press pause on an unrelenting rotation of serving. The traditional short breaks—weekends, vacations, and spa visits—proved insufficient for the soul-deep fatigue that chronic self-sacrifice had ignited. Apparently, women in his practice were going to extremes to find their center, like choosing between their marriages and their well-being. Some simply assumed their partner couldn't or wouldn't meet them halfway. Others had summoned the courage to ask and were handily rejected with uncivilized versions of "This isn't what I signed up for."

This saddened me, and begged the question: What *did* women sign up for? What *did* we want in return for our compounding labors of love? For many, the answer was a thriving professional life, healthy partnership, and peace of mind. In conversations with high-achieving women, and in Dr. Tartt's recounting, the reality of this three-pronged longing was falling far short of the dream.

He said, "Women are opening their laptops at two o'clock in the morning after those full days of exercising, meetings, emails, doing hair, having sex, caring for aging parents, serving the community, and worrying about the state of the world. Men aren't even thinking about all those things."

This take wasn't new, of course, but hearing it this way—especially during an acute attack against women's rights in this country—was triggering. It reminded me of what my friend Soraya Chemaly wrote in her masterpiece *Rage Becomes Her* about women being seen as vessels instead of human beings with agency and whole lives. Honestly, it made me want to burn it all down and move to some small, remote place where people were too busy loving on the land to worry about standing on our necks.

Women who have true partners—people who split chores, bridge gaps, and see themselves as equally responsible for household care and parenting—experience stress differently than those who are default jugglers for every spinning plate. Dr. Tartt illuminated this statistic for me in a simple, stark comparison: On average, married men live two years longer than single men. Women, however, don't benefit from marriage to the same degree and are less happy. *What?*

TIGHTEN UP YOUR BOUNDARIES

We talk a lot about boundaries. Someone taking advantage of you? *Set boundaries.* Too much on your plate? *Set boundaries.* People asking for more than you have to give? *Set boundaries.* But Dr. Tartt rightly pointed out that when everything on your list is important and you're not confident the gaps will be filled without you, setting boundaries feels risky.

He's worked with women who are afraid to push back against the onslaught of expectation because they don't want to "blow up their own spot" or lose what they have—their family, their spouse, their home, their jobs, or their status. I understood that. I'd lived it. He asked what I thought the world would look like if women opted out all at once. I'm seldom at a loss for words, but my brain couldn't do that calculus. Women's work is woven into everything we do, even when we fail to recognize it.

Days later, after I'd had a chance to think, I imagined a less kind, less beautiful, less connected, and less inspiring world, because that's what was looming as the new administration and associates began calling for—and forcing upon us—more masculine energy. On the ground, I envisioned a lot of hungry, dirty, unkempt people who, even as they circumvented huge piles of laundry, still had no idea where their socks were.

More than once, I've overheard my young adult sons in lively conversation with each other, lamenting the quality of the dating pool. "They don't make women like they used to," they say, shaking their heads. *Good,* I think to myself while shaking my own. I'd rather young women start self-possessed and learn to compromise than start selfless and learn the hard way to keep something for themselves. I hope John and I have shown them a different way to partner. Only time will tell.

Back at the resort in Arizona, I considered Jasmine's options.

"Rest," I offered naively, knowing my advice was insufficient—like telling a hungry person to eat or a naked person to put on a shirt. But I didn't necessarily mean that rest would solve her problem. I did believe it would create enough mental space to allow a solution to emerge. Thankfully, she'd orchestrated a sabbatical and was appropriately contemplative about reentry. How could she jump back in with a fresh mindset and at a reasonable pace?

What followed was a passionate debate about overwork. Sasha felt that if she wasn't working, she was standing still. Work brought joy and fulfillment but also created a gravitational pull that occasionally and unexpectedly became a drag, and she was unclear about her tipping point. When I suggested she adjust her high-level approach to get more out of doing less, she bristled. She looked like she smelled a skunk. I chuckled.

"What's the facial expression about? What are you thinking right now?" I asked.

"I don't know," she said, shifting uncomfortably on the edge of the pool. On further exploration, this instinctual response taught her something about herself. She didn't want to work less; she just wanted to be appropriately valued for the work she loves to do and to be able to pause at her discretion without feeling the void.

Overwork had become the norm for Jasmine, initiated by a lifelong battle that began with feeling like the less-beautiful daughter. Accomplishment by accomplishment, she'd been laboring to balance the scales. Each of us wants to feel useful and necessary, and helping—serving—meets this need. The alignment between who we are and what we do provides fuel to keep going and becomes cyclical. But it can be hard to sense your own limits, and just as your body shuts down when it needs the rest you stubbornly refuse to grant, our helper instincts wane too. We talked at length about the trade-offs between the joy of filling the world with goodness and the exhaustion that comes when the container keeps expanding.

We are doers who do until we find ourselves undone. We don't want to be like this, but it's hard to adjust our controls without stopping altogether. Jasmine, Sasha, and I were curious about why. Was it a question of identity? As Black and brown women helpers, who are we if we're not striving, fixing, healing, inspiring, or picking up the slack? Do we know? Can we see ourselves as whole without giving until it's gone? Do we even want to see ourselves without this identity? Do we secretly think less of people who don't lay themselves bare with each sacrifice?

Maybe. But to me, it was also connected to our tainted relationship with achievement, made worse by chronic underestimation. When we set our sights on a goal, we throw everything and the kitchen sink at it. We refuse to be caught short, so we aim higher. And when we reach that higher bar, our first instinct is not to celebrate it but to raise it. When we realize what we're doing, we pound our fists on tables and vow to stop everything all at once. Then we sleep for a week. This is not balance. This is not harmony. It's the most consequential game of tug-of-war we will ever play—a life-preserving battle between winning and well-being.

Conversations like this led me to write this book—not only to share how I reimagined my helper identity and shed some of the weight I was carrying but to offer insights to others trying to do the same. I've solved the overwork problem in my own life, for the most part, by hiring a great team, ensuring my work is valued fairly, and "packaging my genius." But on the days when I do feel overwhelmed, it helps to remember the off-ramp.

I learned about the off-ramp in the Black psychologist's fluffy beige chair. We were discussing my phobia about driving on the freeway. I was twenty-five years old then, and everywhere I drove, I took the long way. I blamed my father for the fact that I didn't get my license until I turned twenty-two. On my first spin behind the wheel, he directed me to the freeway, and we almost got run off the road. That terrifying experience ruined me for years. I'd worked around it but was limiting myself in a myriad of ways, like declining business trips or opting out of gatherings too far for service roads.

"You can always get off," the doctor said with a straight face.

"What do you mean?" I asked, like he was speaking a language I didn't understand. It sounded too simple. *I must be missing something.*

"The freeway," he repeated gently. "You can get on, and if it feels too scary, you can get off."

I refer to this straightforward guidance often. I can try a new thing, take a risk, run a race. If I don't like it, for any reason, I can stop, step back, undo, and get off—whatever feels necessary. This knowing is sometimes the only idea that gives me the courage to do hard things. Even as demands keep rolling in and the air grows thicker with tension, I deserve to feel calm in my body and peace in my spirit. I deserve to be okay. It's the only place from which I can stand strong.

PART III

BEFORE

Clear a Path for Others to Follow

Dear Reader,

Have you ever had a vision greater than your capacity to achieve it?

Have you ever failed to demand your worth?

Do you struggle to narrow all you could do to what you should do?

Have you experienced the pruning process that comes with growth?

Do you fight with perfectionism?

Does the world and all its ills sometimes get you down?

Do you see yourself as a trailblazer but don't want to catch fire?

This part's for you.

Chapter 7

EMERGING

EXPANDING YOUR TERRITORY

"YOU CAN QUIT NOW," my husband announced from just outside my office door one early afternoon in 2017.

"Huh?" I asked, peering over my screen. I was engrossed. My creativity is rhythmic and regimented. Light candle. Strip desk of papers. Organize snacks. Play instrumental jazz or gospel at mid-volume to keep the easily distractible part of my brain busy so the generative part can make magic. John's words didn't register at first.

"Your job. You can quit now. You can go full time on your business."

"Okay," I responded, my eyes wide with a mix of trepidation and glee.

"Okay," he nodded, and walked out.

It was simple, directive, and held all the clarity a sentence could. I knew this meant he'd crunched the numbers, run a multiyear forecast, and done a risk assessment. This is not the kind of thing John would feel *moved* to say. He had to be *informed* to say something like this.

Perfectly still in my ergonomic chair, I inhaled the invitation. I was twenty when I had my very first encounter with Hallmark. I would be forty-two when I had my last. A literal lifetime. I stood—excited and terrified—on the cusp of a new life.

I founded my limited liability company a couple years prior so I could do speaking engagements, small creative writing projects, and the occasional leadership session. But I was still a part-time Hallmark employee, which meant I was making periodic visits to Kansas City while providing co-leadership on an enterprise-wide initiative. In a conversation with John months before, I'd expressed my desire to dive headlong into my business.

I'm often asked why I wanted to be an entrepreneur. I didn't. I left my corporate job because I wasn't ready to cap my potential and the right and necessary move to Texas interrupted my trajectory. Though my professional reputation and relationships gave me immense freedom, the job I held rang hollow when there was nothing left to strive for. Beginning again meant striving again, and I needed to feel that feeling—to challenge my creative limits and to reach for my edge. Little did I know that my experience at Hallmark would become the foundation of everything I'd soon build.

Around the time John announced the arrival of my professional freedom train, I found myself in the balcony at the Potter's House in Dallas, Texas, listening for spiritual guidance on how to move forward. Senior pastor Bishop T. D. Jakes said something that changed the way I viewed work. He told a story about a stranger who—recognizing that Jakes was writing books, plays, and movies, hosting a television show, pastoring a church, and building a philanthropy platform—asked how he manages to do "all those things." After considering the question, Bishop expressed that he doesn't do "all those things." He does one thing. He uses the power of story to change lives.

This resonated, and I made it my business to clarify my one thing. What was inherently true and transferable about my gifts, my philosophy, my passion, and my expertise? I began to imagine my future as less about a job title or industry expertise and more about the experience I'd gained and the impact I wanted to have. This shift meant my value wouldn't be defined by executive leadership or greeting cards but by all the things I cared about and now knew how to do. This included visioning, consumer understanding and insight, product development, creative strategy and execution, talent management, cultural competence, business innovation, and more.

My building blocks were enviable, but I still had to arrange them. I'll admit here that not much of my professional life since has been a surprise to me. It's been delightful, rewarding, and overwhelming in a good way. But not surprising.

I was twenty-five when I started managing people. There were twenty-two creatives on my team, and some had been at the company longer than I'd been alive. Weeks into the new job, a team member showed up at my door and asked if he could share something with me.

"Of course," I said. "Come on in." He sat down in the chair across from mine, relaxed into it, and set his hands on his knees.

"God showed me something about you, and I feel moved to share it, if that's okay," he began, confirming that conveying the message was still acceptable, now that I understood the nature of it. I knew David was deeply religious. I also knew he was considered somewhat of a prophet, though he kept that close to the vest.

"Go on. Please," I invited. I was hoping that whatever he had to say would help me navigate all the great expectations attached to my new job.

But that wasn't it.

"God showed me your future," he said. I sat back in my chair and rubbed my thumbs to my forefingers—an unconscious relaxation behavior. I didn't know where he was going with this.

"I saw you on stage in front of thousands of people. Above your head was a sign with your name on it. In lights." He swiped his hand above his own head to mimic what he saw. "The crowd was filled with people who've been left behind—God's people who have struggled to be seen and heard. Who've been forgotten. You were leading them toward something. You were giving them hope."

This was the first but not the last time David would prophesy to me, and when he did, he'd insert "Does that make sense?" between each main idea. Considering the facts of my life then, it did not make sense. I had a new job, a new husband, and a new baby. Nothing about my reality suggested a future like the one he described. I thanked him, and he went on his way.

Approximately ten years later, I graced my first stage. Twenty-two years later, I published *The Waymakers*. It's been twenty-five years since David showed up at my office door, and while I've not yet seen my name in lights, the rest is a very real part of a story that's still being written.

It can take time to pave the way to your purpose, and the beginning of my helper journey was bumpy at best. Betting on myself after building such a successful corporate career was energizing and, at the same time, unnerving. What if I didn't make any money? What if once I shed the big brand associated with my name, no one wanted to hire me? This fear of being perceived as a nobody led me to significantly undervalue my work at first.

It wasn't all in my head. The value dynamics were real. There was "Hallmark Tara," who led Mahogany and multicultural strategy and worked with Dr. Maya Angelou, and then there was Tara Jaye Frank, standing solo—without the brand, influence, connections, or budget. I was once offered a magazine feature in recognition of my accomplishments. I accepted, but when I updated my employment status, they rescinded the offer. They didn't really want to recognize me—they just wanted Hallmark to pay for an advertisement and a gala table. These moments felt awful. You go from being the person everyone wants something from to the person people assume wants something from them. From professional princess to pariah overnight.

It was a slow start. An author friend said she made $400,000 per year speaking and teaching women's leadership development programs, and she believed I could do it too. Money like that would replace my Hallmark income, but I wasn't sure how to begin. I stumbled my way forward, sharing thought leadership on LinkedIn as a springboard.

When people ask about my greatest lessons as an entrepreneur, I tell them there were two big ones I learned early on. One was the criticality of focus. When you first step onto the small business path, at least in services, you're flexible. You're not sure what will resonate or what clients will pay for, so you pitch your tent in the land of everything. The problem is that clients won't give major projects to people who aren't experts. While flexibility helps at first, it can quickly become a liability. Learning what I was uniquely good at and knowing what I *wanted* to do, as opposed to what I *could* do, guided my later choices and investments.

The second is to avoid the trap of caring more about a solution than a client's problem. As a creative person, I'd make something and, believing it was beautiful, insist on selling my beautiful thing. I didn't spend enough time understanding the opportunity through the client's lens. After several lost bids, I flipped that paradigm and began asking better questions and listening more intentionally. I stopped trying to sell my wares and worked to develop meaningful solutions that met real needs.

These two principles, along with a committed operations partner in the early days that eventually grew into a committed team, brought a fitting end to the no-win game of entrepreneurial whack-a-mole. I began thinking differently about expanding my territory and started saying no to business opportunities I didn't want or wasn't equipped for so I could prioritize difference-making work. Casting my net too wide led to wasted effort. In time, I figured out how to set myself and the team up for greater success.

If you feel disappointed in your own path or just confused about what to do now, know that where you go from here depends on your ability to embrace who you are and honor your gifts and experiences. What sets you apart? What lights you on fire? What are you naturally good at? What do people who know you best see in you that you don't see? What steps have you taken toward the goal that keeps calling you to it? And when you take those steps, who is cheering you on? In an extremely crowded market, it helps to answer the "Why you?" question before the "Why that?" one.

Expanding your territory is about being open to your own potential. This is what turning fifty gave me. Permission to journey without waiting on arrival. To play without fixating on winning. To make decisions about my life and work, then undecide if I feel like it. To see the universe of possibility as mine to explore, to be enriched by, to hold—but not be beholden to.

STAND ON YOUR ROCK

"You have to stop speaking for so little money," my business mentor mandated during my first year solo after it slipped that I was charging $5,000 for a keynote speech.

"I'm new at this," I responded, pleading my case. "I'm still building a reputation outside my former company. If I make the barrier to entry low for those who want to hire me, I can build credibility. Plus, I'm making a difference."

"You are *not* new at this. You've had a twenty-year corporate career. You are a gifted speaker. You know things others don't know and have accomplished things others have not accomplished. And you can make a difference without selling yourself short."

I understood his point, but felt I had to work up to higher fees. I nodded my head to appease him. He saw right through it.

"Let me put it this way," he continued. "Every time you speak for such little money, you set the bar low for others who need to make a living doing this—people who may not even be as good as you are. If they can get Tara Jaye Frank for $5,000, why would they pay someone else ten thousand? Or twenty thousand? Or more?" He went on to list speaker fees for men he knew who had similar experience. The numbers made my head spin.

I squirmed when he said my name that way: *Tara Jaye Frank*. It sounded like someone else. Someone more important. This, of course, was part of my problem.

I hadn't thought about fees in the way he explained it—as harming the market and my colleagues, as compromising others' chances of being valued fairly. As a helper, this idea mortified me. I increased my prices that day, but years later, I considered why undervaluing myself wasn't enough of a reason to change. I wondered why it took activating my helper instinct to move me to action. This reflection didn't feel good, and as I refined my business model, I pushed myself to define fair value and muster the courage to lose business if that's what fairness required.

This entire concept took me back to my one thing. I needed to identify my rock so that I could polish it and stand on it confidently—and so that if I must be agile as my business grew, I would never stray too far from my core competence or credibility.

I tried a few ideas on for size in a conversation with a former colleague.

"My work is about helping people be successful," I said, smiling.

She cocked her head to the side. "Too broad. Says nothing of what distinguishes you."

"I use my creativity to help people be successful." I laughed. It was a lazy edit.

This went on for a while until I keyed into two dominant threads that seemed to follow me all my life: building bridges and being incredibly creative. I was at my best when I deeply understood the reality of something, could envision it in its most evolved state, and used my creativity to get from point A to point B. With some iteration, I landed on a professional rock that has guided me ever since: *I build bridges between people and ideas.*

Clarifying this one thing meant I *would* do work that connected people to each other. It meant I *would* construct solutions that didn't already exist to achieve worthy outcomes. And it meant I *would not* do anything to divide, destroy, or deteriorate people, places, or potential.

From that day forward, I would harness care, connection, creativity, and courage to transform workplaces and equip leaders to lead better. My rock fit every professional whim of mine and, at the same time, provided guardrails. I felt clear, confident, and anchored in place—mostly. Of course, I've had to weather the occasional storm since, and some of my own making.

DITCH PERFECTION

Even when life is good, my Virgo tendencies get triggered and I cause needless problems for myself. My experience with writing

Emerging

and publishing my first book, *The Waymakers,* is a perfect example of my tussle with discontentment.

Full disclosure: I wrote the book with high hopes of making bestsellers' lists. Author friends warned me against focusing on this goal. They said it was a moving target and that—with few exceptions—the publishing industry chooses the books they want to elevate. With proverbial fingers in my ears, I invested heavily in the goal. I hired an experienced public relations firm, devised an elaborate launch plan with one hundred high-end book boxes that included custom-designed Waymakers products, and paid to print twenty-five thousand copies of my book, even though the hybrid publisher recommended we start with two thousand five hundred. I knew it sounded crazy, but I believed this book would be important. It held clear answers to the questions so many leaders were asking about equity and inclusion, and my clients were large companies with hundreds of thousands of employees. Four members of my team were dedicated to this effort for six months prior to launch while I delivered keynotes and trainings and ran the podcast circuit. To date, we've sold more than sixteen thousand copies of *The Waymakers,* so I really wasn't *that* crazy.

I spared no expense—and I didn't make one list. I'd sold a few thousand copies leading up to and during launch week, but due to a miscommunication between my publishing partner, the distributor, and a bookseller, they weren't counted. I was devastated and admittedly frustrated by what appeared to be inattention, incompetence, or both. After publication, I obsessively compared my book's success to that of others. If it was ranked higher than a similar book on Monday, I felt satisfied. If it slipped by Tuesday, I was crushed.

My emotionally regulated moments sounded like: *What if it weren't reasonable to expect a bestseller on the first go? What can I learn from this experience? What might I do differently next time, if anything?* But mostly, discontentment had me in a stranglehold: *Why not me? My book is just as good as (fill in the blank)! It's because I'm not famous! Waaahhh!*

To ground me, friends shared how unusual it is for a self- or hybrid-published book to make the lists. Rationalization didn't help. I'd run against odds before and conquered enough professional mountains to believe my experience could be different. It was not. And the disappointment was almost more than I could stand. My team knew I felt disappointed, but I tried to conceal just how much. They made magic happen leading up to publication and beyond. I was proud of what we created together, and they deserved to be proud too. My preoccupation with recognition would temper the enthusiasm they earned the right to feel.

A month after *The Waymakers* launched, my husband walked into the kitchen to find me sitting at the island in tears.

"T, what's going on?" He caught me while I was feeling most sorry for myself. *Peak sorry.*

"I worked so hard on this book," I said. "I spent so much money. I focused months of my team's time on it. I paid for twenty-five thousand copies. I poured everything I had into it, and it wasn't enough. I feel like a failure."

His response shook me. I don't know what I expected him to say, but it wasn't this.

"Don't you dare," he said. "Do *not* do that." He was shaking his head *and* his finger.

Startled, I raised my head from the dark hole I'd created by wrapping my arms around it and peeked at him from the corner of my eye. The engineer had arrived to deconstruct my pity party. Invitation or no invitation, he was ripping up the dance floor.

"This book is amazing," he said. "Those who've read it, love it. You're helping people, and whether it's one person or one million, your work is having an impact. Don't discount every good thing you've accomplished because you missed some invisible bar that no one can even clearly define for you. Stop it."

Stop it? What am I, five?

I let out a deep, guttural sigh and threw my head back. *Very five-ish.* This self-deprecating cycle of setting an audacious goal, throwing everything I have at it, missing it by a hair (or a head full of hair, in this case), then failing to recognize all that I'd learned and gained in the process was a poorly morphed version of the mindset that limited me when I was young. I'd only try what I knew I could master. I'd only compete in contests I was sure I'd win. I'd only apply for opportunities I was confident I'd get. And when I didn't think I would succeed at something, I acted wholly disinterested in it to mask my fear of failure. The winning I'd experienced in my young adult life may have appeared extraordinary to others, but it was calculated and de-risked. For reasons I may never fully understand, I wasn't happy when I was great—only when I was better. *Ouch.*

As I matured, I worked hard to push myself beyond this childish protection mechanism, and *The Waymakers* was among the most material long shots I'd taken in my life. Falling short made me want to cross my arms, stomp my feet, and retreat to my safe space. At least I could control the narrative in there. To this day, I take no five-star review, no book recommendation, and no unsolicited words of praise for granted. They all mean something to me. They all remind me why I do the work I do, especially now.

Social media makes these self-incriminating tendencies worse. We compare ourselves and our accomplishments with other people's best days. Most don't post about the call they didn't get or the project that was rejected. They don't announce the end of their romantic relationships (unless they're *big* famous). They post media appearances but leave out that they're struggling to pay their bills. They share their new job offer and neglect to mention the many months they spent submitting applications. And even if everything another person touches turns to gold, that doesn't mean there's not something just as meaningful and valuable waiting for you. Contentment can't be cultivated through filters and hashtags. Every scroll serves up countless reasons to feel bad about ourselves if we leave our minds ajar for the portion.

We live in a society that feigns perfection—that commoditizes everything we know (and even what we don't know) and has young people genuinely believing they're one viral video from millionaire status. We're bombarded with the idea that a good vision board or lock-tight formula or two-part course is all we need to make a great life. And, sadly, when we're not yet leading the life we want, we think we're doing it wrong.

While there are certainly bright stars who have made quantum leaps in their careers, it doesn't work that way for most people. Life can change in an instant, but right now I'm objectively successful. We have few liabilities. I'm free. I can choose who I work with. I can take time off when I want to. I can say what I feel is right and true without fear. I need for nothing and have most of what I want. I don't say any of this to brag; I say it because there was no shortcut to this place. I didn't grow up with money or inherited power. There were long hours, risks, failures, and many stubs of the toe. There were rejections, corrections, underestimations, and painful, expensive, and sometimes repetitive lessons. And as you now know, there was trauma.

A good life is not all spotlights and epiphanies. More often, it unfolds one brave step at a time. Meaning is found in your own circuitous journey and in the bought lessons of others whose stories shed light on the mountains worth climbing, the detours worth taking, and the potholes to avoid. It is beyond time for us to ditch perfection and reclaim our humanness with our faith and foibles in tow. Because while we may look at others' lives and want what they have, what we can't see is how they got there—the shadows they worked to evade and the many lessons they're still learning every day.

One chilly Florida morning, I walked into a local coffee shop to order my customary lavender almond-milk latte. A jar in front of the register wore a sign that said "Morning inspiration: Please take one." I did, and the small, folded piece of paper read "A minute's success pays the failure of years," a quote by Robert Browning.

I folded it back up and put it in my purse.

I firmly believe we give up too fast because we forget that failing is part of succeeding. We exchange money for things we're destined to discover. I know I have. I've redefined success as freedom, and I'm learning to normalize having it unfold with time, intentionality, experience, and iteration. Constantly scanning the horizon for shortcuts left me carrying exhausting levels of hypervigilance. It reduced my ability to enjoy the journey. And it made me forget that I am indeed before the world and its jewels.

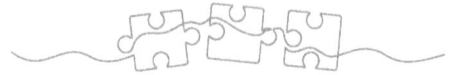

Chapter 8

GROWING UP

BE DISCIPLINED

IN A MEETING SCHEDULED to kick off the work year, I promised my team "No new babies," meaning we'd stop investing in additional solutions when we hadn't yet "raised" the ones we'd launched. As a process pioneer, I like generating ideas. Exercising the discipline required to sustain a thing doesn't come as naturally to me as creating it. For me, creativity is life, and harnessing the skills and talents of others to create something that feels novel and necessary makes work fun.

When I first started my company, The Waymakers Change Group, about a decade ago, I brainstormed a long list of ideas for how our value proposition could come to life, including services, products, events, certifications, and an online learning management system. Our work uses data, experiential learning, and systems enhancements to close the contribution gap between employee performance and employee potential, and there were so many possible paths into the work. Seven years later, I realized I was running down the list like something was chasing me. This was problematic for many reasons. We weren't improving what we'd already created. The return on investment was low because I'd shift our attention before we could extract it. And I was unable to fine-tune my team's capability and composition in ways that made us better at getting the most important work done faster. New ideas meant new skill sets, new processes, and new expenses. It was exciting but woefully inefficient. Most days felt like starting over.

I wish I had a better explanation for why it took me so long to course correct. The easy answer is that doing what I love is energizing and doing what I don't love is draining and hard to sustain. But I also felt pressure to stay ahead in a race that was mostly in my mind. Trying to be everywhere, doing everything all at once, had never worked for me. Yet somewhere along the path, I'd allowed the constant buzz of outside activity to convince me otherwise. If a colleague started a podcast, I wondered if I should restart mine. When people began selling courses, I thought I should do the same. In fact, I invested tens of thousands of dollars and six solid months of my team's time building a learning management system that failed miserably. Each time I revved the engine on something new, I grew more overwhelmed. More babies meant more care and feeding. And in my world, care and feeding meant software licensing costs, personnel, vendors, time, money, and attention—all of which distracted us from mastering the work that set us apart: the 20 percent our clients relied on us for because we were "differently good" at it.

The answer to our elevation was there, but it was buried beneath sparkle and shine, thanks to my lack of discipline. I'd just decided to exit the learning management system when I brought my team together in person to talk about the future. Exiting was a tough call, considering the sunk cost and immense lift it took to build it, but I knew we couldn't keep going down the wrong road just because we'd been on it for a while. All eight people on my team had made important contributions to the business with their resourcefulness, talent, insight, experience, and attention to detail—their sheer passion. We sat in a conference room for two days, walking through our current workload, painstakingly reviewing what was and wasn't working, and sharing ideas for how we could be more disciplined in our mission to help all people contribute freely, fully, and fairly.

I kept repositioning myself in the chair, my right hand gripping a pen that I used to doodle on a piece of paper, and the left, playing with my hair. Kas once asked if I have attention deficit hyperactivity disorder. I said no, because I've never been diagnosed. But the longer I live and work, the more resonant the associated behaviors seem. One Thanksgiving, while several family members gathered around the kitchen island reminiscing about our childhoods, my mother recalled how stressed my high school study habits made her.

"I'd tell you to do your homework and, minutes later, find you sitting with the radio or television on, a sketchpad to your right, a book open, and your homework scattered on the surface in front of you. And I'd think, 'There's no way she can concentrate like this!' But you'd just say, 'I'm doing it!' And you always got it done. I believed you could get even better grades if you tried harder. But you didn't care about grades. You cared about the experience. I didn't understand it then."

She could have told that same story about every day of my professional life. Order—at least how most define it—is not my strength. I'm an organic, circular thinker and maker. I'm planful but not organized. Analytical but not methodical. A conversation with me before I've had a chance to gather my thoughts can be disorienting. And yet I've discovered that few can synthesize information and paint a mental picture quite like me. Few can take that picture and deconstruct it into actionable parts quite like me. Few can speak to hearts and minds in a compelling, unscripted sequence quite like me. Learning to harness my brain's natural operating system and the unique gifts I've been granted to create value *is* my superpower. I'll never be a master of systems, schedules, or processes, and my to-do lists are mostly for show. But as a business owner, I respect the role of order in enhancing my creativity. And I knew I had to get more disciplined about simplifying what I *could* master: solutions.

I'd invited my husband John, who serves as our executive advisor, to the meeting. He saw our growth path right away and suggested we lead with our 20 percent—our proprietary diagnostic that ties employee experiences to business outcomes and identifies priority actions. *Know what matters.* He also brought a no-nonsense lens to the waste that was getting in our way. *Do what counts.*

I spent the next few months refining that core value. I converged products I'd created and had been delivering for years into a comprehensive methodology that would allow us to assess, design for, and measure workplace culture change more effectively. The helper in me genuinely wanted to get results for my clients, not just make them feel good or check boxes. This was the work—the merging, refining, and packaging of my genius—that made way for licensing and train-the-trainer solutions, which transformed my business and increased our deal size by more than ten times in six months.

This exponential evolution had less to do with new ideas and more to do with the discipline to prioritize what was most needed, most valuable, and most differentiated. And the discipline to stop doing what wasn't. We became more intentional about leading with the difference-making work instead of the fifty things we *could* do, *might* do, or *would be willing* to do. We pointed our resources toward revenue-driving activity and streamlined our overhead expense. And we finalized and aligned our pricing strategy so we could stop negotiating our value out of fear that we'd leave money on the table—a dance that sucked us dry.

Of course, it's not just business that requires greater discipline from us. It's everything else we do too, like our involvement in organizations, committees, groups, and clubs. When you're a helper, people want you to participate in everything. You agree—until parts of you are strewn like leaves in a windstorm—random, separate, and far from the root.

For me, figuring out how I can *best* help—if I can at all—has been a lifesaver. I can provide feedback on a concept, a piece of writing, or a pricing strategy. I can share your good ideas with my network. I can make a warm introduction to a fellow helper who will support you in tangible ways. But being disciplined means saving my energy for what matters and doing what counts in all corners of my world—helping when and where I can, *effectively*. This mindset and approach have allowed me to show up as a better and happier version of myself everywhere I go.

DO WHAT YOU GOTTA DO—FOR YOU

On a sunny Florida day in the summer of 2024, my oldest brother, Todd, lay perfectly relaxed in the beach lounger next to mine, listening as I verbally processed options that might help my business withstand the rising anti-DEI sentiment. The struggle was real. Some colleagues were shuttering their firms. Others were taking their companies down to the studs, meaning them and their stand-in email addresses. We still had a healthy client roster, but it had fallen eerily silent. It was like *Night of the Comet*—the 1984 science-fiction movie where neighbors go outside to watch a once-in-a-lifetime celestial event and turn into red dust or zombies. Some projects had been obliterated. *Red dust.* Others were moving slow and dragging one leg, murmuring all the way. *Zombies.* We were hiding in the studio with our valuables tucked in our arms and our ears to the door.

The market was undeniably shifting, and even opportunities I believed would eventually pull through had been temporarily paused. I was considering changing my employment model to reduce financial risk, but I was torn about what it could mean for team members and partners I really cared about. Building a company founded on helping is rewarding. The responsibility that comes with it is a mixed bag, especially when your work is predicated on a lightning-rod issue.

"Do what you have to do for you and your family," Todd said, with more assertiveness than the moment seemed to call for.

"I get that."

"No," he said adamantly. "Let me tell you something." He sat up straight from a reclining position and swung his 222-pound frame around to face me.

"Sharon"—his wife's mother—"built her business, right?" His hands were already waving in the air, poised to emphasize his points. "Her business was *very* successful. *Very.* She hired a bunch of people and paid them good money. She promoted them and gave them opportunities to take on bigger roles. They loved her. 'Sharon this' and 'Sharon that.' This woman could do no wrong, Tara."

He pronounced my name "TAH-ra," with a short *a*, because living in Florida for thirty years hadn't erased his New England accent the way Atlanta, then Kansas City, then Dallas had erased mine.

He went on. "So then Covid hits and the business struggles. People weren't leaving their houses, so she had to let people go.

They were *pissed*. All that love and praise went out the window." Sweeping arm motions now.

I nodded my head, humming the yeses in all the right places to make sure he knew I was paying close attention.

"*Then!*" he shouts. "She gets cancer. And all those people were nowhere to be found. Not one of them came to see her, offered to help, nothing. They were just gone. So *you* do what *you* need to do for *you* and *your* family. That's it." Hands thrown in the air. An exclamation point on a very pragmatic sentence.

You.

It's a word I still struggled with. People in helping professions don't think much of themselves beyond what they give away. We expect to make sacrifices and compromises. We expect to be uncomfortable and inconvenienced. We expect to be selfless and, in many cases, see it as a responsibility and privilege. We even expect, though never invite, occasional abuse.

My mother-in-love was an infectious disease nurse for fifty years. Recently, while walking to the same beach where my brother tried to shake sense into me, she told me about how early in her career, a white male patient refused her care.

"I walked into his hospital room to introduce myself, and he asked for the nurse," she said, each word careful and deliberate. "I told him that I was his nurse. '*You* are a nurse practitioner?' he questioned." It was the 1970s, and she was the only Black nurse at the hospital.

"So I smiled and responded, 'Why yes, I am.' He insisted on being treated by a different nurse. 'I understand,' I said to him. 'I'm happy to talk to the nurse in charge for you.' When I relayed his request to the nurse in charge, she didn't want to accommodate him. She said it wasn't right. But he was the sick one. He was the patient. And if he wanted different care, I believed that he should have that."

As I listened to her story, I felt the heat rise in my body. Selfless even when doubted, disrespected, and dismissed. Selfless when subjugated. *Always selfless.*

It was easy for me to cut ties in certain situations. For instance, I decided years before that I wouldn't work with companies whose CEOs do not believe inequity exists. I refused to be the great persuader. Instead, I sought to work with companies who believe in the *why* of equitable and inclusive leadership but need help with the *how*. *How* is where we thrive. *How* is our gift to the world. If external factors compromise my ability to do meaningful work, they must go. But people I love and care about? That's a very different story.

Todd—perhaps more hard-lined than my personality would permit—was right. Business leaders make tough calls all the time, and while these decisions feel very personal and are difficult to overcome, they can't always be avoided. I'd spent countless hours considering how the lives of team members might be impacted if I changed my employment model and very little time thinking about what would happen to my life if I didn't. Was it because I knew my husband and I had more options? Maybe. But why was I willing to sacrifice the business I'd been building for ten years to avoid disappointing people? Why would I default to my own discomfort to keep everyone else comfortable? Why would I consider letting my help hurt me and my family?

Most people I've invited to work with me over the years—whether as employees, independent contractors, or vendors—were in transition somehow. They were starting something new and needed a boost. They experienced a job loss. They were unhappy at work. They were trying to figure out what to do next, and working with me brought clarity. They needed more money to meet their family obligations. I'd built a team, quite literally, with my helper instinct. I was proud of that, and every person I've worked alongside has earned their keep. They were good hires at the time of hiring, but when circumstances changed, I struggled to change with them. I didn't want to hurt the people I had helped.

Thankfully, due to a few strategic shifts, I was able to preserve and even enhance The Waymakers without too many casualties. There *were* casualties, however—lines I had to cut. I did so with as much empathy as possible, but I didn't escape the Sharon effect. I was the bad guy—the one who took something away, even though I was also the one who gave it. These conflicts can compel us to stop giving altogether. When people rely on the help you provide, you can't always quietly sunset that help. You can't always lift it or shift it. Sometimes the only way to save yourself is to cut the line.

Trust the Process

A year after John and I married and blended our families, we moved into our current home, a two-story with enough space for us and our six children to live comfortably. Days after moving in, John hung a poster on the garage wall much like one his father had given him decades before. In the center was a modern house atop a sunset hill. Three exotic cars sat in the driveway, and in the background—a private jet. For a boy who used his parents' blanket-covered legs as roads for his fifty-plus car collection when he was three, the poster served as inspiration, illuminating what was possible and inviting him to dream big. Since then, for the most part, my husband's path has been propelled by one bold visualization after another. He sees a goal in his mind's eye, deconstructs it, works some parts alone, then together with others, attains the goal, and starts again. For him, dreaming is never just dreaming. It's more like planning with bravado.

A few years before we moved into that house, when we'd first started dating, we went for walks on the plot of land where our house now stands. There wasn't yet a road—just a clearing with piles of soil and stone. The stage was set for neighborhood expansion, and while we liked the developer's plans, neither of us had the means to do much about it. On one of these walks, I picked up a small stone and dropped it in my pocket. When we returned to the house we were temporarily living in, I set the stone on the bathroom counter. Every morning I noticed it, and so did John. When the developer began contracting for new builds, we applied for a loan. At the time, it was a stretch, especially considering the financial harm inflicted by my divorce. We jumped through hoop after hoop, and thanks to John's vision and persistence, we closed on that house and moved our family into it in 2014. This was just one of many shared life achievements that began with a vision, evolved with a plan, and concluded with a miracle.

There are countless dreams that have come true because I first dared to dream them. My twenty-one-year Hallmark career. My remarriage. My consulting business. My last book and this one—seeing it, listening to that still, small voice, and aligning my good works with an openness to divine guidance.

A decade ago, I heard God say, "Tell them how I restored you." My restoration story has been—if I consider every ordered step—a lesson in miracles. I tried to write several books before this one, but every time I attempted to unpack the story of my divorce, I got stuck. I was still healing, and my children were too young. It occurred to me while in conversation with Elaine Lin Hering, a friend who wrote the book *Unlearning Silence*, that the seed is not the harvest. While the seed was planted long ago, it took a decade for this book to gestate and just six weeks to be born.

I recognize the situations explored in *You Are Before the World* happened to more than just me, but the stories are mine. No one experienced them the way I did. No one learned what I learned or used the loose threads to form what I have formed. It took me many years to own my version of the truth as something

I have a right to represent on my terms. But I've learned there's power in story. My lessons are not just mine. Your lessons are not just yours. This "lone wolf" idea that we must make our way through every wilderness solo has us feeling less wild and free and more worn and faint.

Before the iteration of this book that you're reading now, I was writing a business book about cultivating cross-boundary relationships. This is part of my job, and the stories I wrote were of times I extended myself to form connections—and to facilitate them—with and between people who didn't have much in common. My firm has helped people find their way to more respectful, harmonious relationships at work so they can get more done and experience greater joy doing it. I believed the ability to meet this need would become more important, not less. I also felt that professionals would benefit from learning what I've learned—from doing what I've taught. I wanted this to be a "big" book, so I hired a book proposal coach whose team helped me shape something that would be attractive to major publishers. We added stories that might expand the book's appeal—examples of grace giving, trust granting, and risk taking and accounts of times I offered *many* benefits of *many* doubts and encouraged others to do the same. While not especially provocative, it was a respectable body of work.

When the proposal was finished, the coach helped me secure a reputable agent, and the agent pitched the book to dozens of publishers. Weeks passed as I held my breath, waiting to learn about my options. My head was following the formula. My heart watched from the sidelines—nervous and unsure.

Three publishers expressed interest, and I selected one to help me bring the book to life. I started writing, but in the months leading up to the 2024 election, my creative flow came to a screeching halt. Even parts I'd once loved now read as overly simplistic, and the advice I'd given leaders time and again fell flat on the page.

My spirit was irritated. The book and its contents felt like a sweater you loved on the model but couldn't stop itching in. Day after day, I'd pour myself a cup of coffee. Light my candle. Arrange my snacks. Turn on my instrumental focus tunes. Sit in front of my laptop. And stare desperately at pages on pages of content I no longer loved. I knew it was over when I stopped feeling personally compelled to do what the book aimed to encourage. To put it plainly, I had no interest in contorting myself so strangers would love and respect me, and I couldn't ask anyone whose life experience mirrored mine to do so either—at least, not leading up to and through the watershed moment I sensed was upon us.

After having invested more than six months, tens of thousands of dollars (yes, I've made many expensive mistakes!), and forty thousand words, I called my literary agent and told him I'd decided to sideline the business book. Immediately, I began writing a new, more personal work that I initially called *See the Light*. The plan was to gather stories and light practices from people all over the world to help the rest of us see our way through dark times. I envisioned traveling to new and different locations—my own *Eat, Pray, Love* sabbatical of sorts. It was soothing to think about and hopeful to talk about. Who doesn't love light? Who hasn't experienced darkness? But it was safe. In planning to tell everyone else's stories, I was hiding from my own unearthing.

I sat down again one fall morning to write the book, and vignette by vignette, *You Are Before the World* took shape. Friends cautioned me about withholding my accelerators—the biggest lessons I learned the hardest way, like the moments I spent on my knees, the leaps I took, and the mistakes I made.

The fears I had and have still—all of which laid the foundation on which abundance has been built.

I didn't know if, at this point in my life, exchanging privacy for potential impact was wise. After all, writers never really know if what they've written resonates until someone reads it. You throw your heart against a wall and see what sticks. This trepidation was amplified by the fact that I am simply me—an ordinary person with an extraordinary life in which extraordinary is not defined by followers, fame, praise, or recognition.

The process I'm trusting now, even as I write, is the discovery process. I'm trusting the reality that there are many more people who have climbed—and are still climbing—their way to a life of significance than there are who've skyrocketed there or been placed there by benefactors. I'm trusting that wanting to be before the world is more common an experience than having it manipulated for your gain.

I've found extraordinariness on the other side of curiosity—in seeking, trying, failing, and trying again. In giving, loving, and serving. And in learning how—with each step forward, backward, and away—to put myself before the world. As I continue to shape this book, I'm believing that your longing to be human will recognize my longing to be human. That you'll be inspired and compelled by both the ordinary and extraordinary moments I've chosen to share with you. That you'll see yourself in me, and me in you, and know that we are—all of us—before the world. Our misguided frame that any one person is more or less than another has muddied our spirits. To me, this is one of the greatest lies ever told—that God's children share one narrowly defined story and that there are millions, if not billions, of people whose stories do not count.

We're here now, together, because I feel called to remind givers that the world is both your helping ground and your harvest ground. Everything is possible. We find our way to a life of significance not by following a blueprint but by remaining open to what life insists on teaching us, no matter how many times we run from the lesson. As a person who battles feelings of anxiety every day, I'm learning to be still—to stop chasing wisdom and instead let it fall on me.

When I reflect on my fifty years on this planet, I see God's hand in every major transition in my life. There were times it was easy to trust the process and other times I tried to control the uncontrollable. Still, every moment has been carefully nested. A challenge couldn't be conquered until a lesson was learned. A win couldn't be appreciated until something was lost. I got what I needed when I needed it, and the frustration I sometimes felt believing God was late—or worse, absent—caused me unnecessary pain.

Earlier, in chapter 3, I referenced the almost $80,000 check I wrote to settle the massive real estate debt left unresolved from my divorce. At first I tried paying the mortgages. Then I attempted to negotiate payoff arrangements, but there were so many banks that the combined amounts would have put me under. The banks showed no mercy. I'd guaranteed the loans. If needed, they planned to garnish my wages to get their money back. Pleasant requests became forceful demands, then turned into pointed threats. I was buckling, and one night, after months of fielding nonstop calls at work and at home, I fell to my knees in a heap of groans and sobs. At a loss, I cried out for God to help me.

The next day, I hired an attorney to intercede on my behalf. He was able to negotiate all the balances—equal to almost $1 million—down to a combined $75,000. Although I didn't have $75,000, I was hopeful because our executive bonuses were supposed to pay out that year.

A couple weeks later, I walked into a large conference room filled with more than one hundred of my peers who, like me, were waiting to hear details about our payout. I found a seat along the back wall and placed my notepad and pen in my lap. When the results were announced, I immediately began calculating on my notepad. When all was said and done, I received a net payout of just over $80,000—a few thousand more than what I owed the banks. Holding on to either side of my chair, I struggled to stifle the sounds of gratitude rising in me and left the room to collect myself. I couldn't believe it, and yet it was par for the course. *He may not come when you want Him, but He'll be there right on time. Trust the process.*

Little did I know that due to a surreal turn of events on the evening of November 5, 2024, there'd be a lot more trusting required.

PART IV

THE WORLD

People Are More Important Than Systems

Dear Reader,

    Are your values being challenged?

    Have you ever lost your way?

    Do you feel chronically disappointed with the world and the people in it?

    Do you know you're meant to facilitate change but unsure how?

    Are you still trying to recognize God's hand in your life?

    This part's for you.

Chapter 9

LEADING THROUGH THE WILDERNESS

CREATING SAFETY

I THOUGHT ABOUT QUITTING. IN the weeks following the 2024 election, when guns came blazing against everything I'd worked for, believed in, and built, I considered walking away. From diversity, equity, and inclusion work. From my business. From everything connected to corporate culture. I didn't know toward what exactly, but it was clear that the already hard work associated with fairness and inclusion would get harder. It did. And in the very beginning, I just wasn't sure I wanted to keep pushing the boulder up the hill. This was no longer an anti-DEI sentiment; it was an all-out assault. I was war-torn enough.

When Socrates first spoke the phrase "You are before the world" and I stood in the breezeway considering its many angles, the third interpretation—*people are before systems*—planted a powerful seed in me. That seed led to a reconciliation of the many conflicting feelings I'd been cycling through since my eyes popped open on November 6.

The idea affirmed the premise behind my last book, *The Waymakers*, which is that while systems impact outcomes, it's people who create, propagate, resist, and dismantle systems. A wide view of America's rapid remaking was all the evidence we needed to know how true this is. On the generative side, individual leaders—and groups of individuals who share similar values and priorities—have the power to open doors, remove barriers, and usher people through to greater levels of contribution. It's the daily choices we make and the behaviors we exhibit that make fairness and inclusion possible.

Beyond the strategic implications, though, the concept of people being before systems felt very personal. Spiritual, even. In my work with The Waymakers, the practical frameworks I'd painstakingly created took a backseat to the emotions running through and between the people I encountered. These emotions were predominantly frustration, anger, doubt, mistrust, and sadness. I believed that what businesses needed most in this perilous climate were people who would work together across boundaries to solve the many interconnected problems that continued to arise. Teamwork, innovation, and discretionary effort were antidotes to the chaos. Unfortunately, none of these can thrive in a hope-starved environment.

These days, before I enter any professional space, I first pause to ground myself. I pray that God inhabits my thoughts, my words, my heart, and my spirit. Some situations require more power than I alone possess, and I've begun to see myself as less of an expert and more of a vessel. I never know who I'll meet in these rooms or how much resistance I might face. A colleague on LinkedIn who's worked in diversity, equity, and inclusion for decades recently questioned how I'm still standing.

"Sometimes I sit," I replied with a smile.

Leadership means different things to different people, and not all leaders see the work they do as service. Some just like money and influence. For those who really care about people—who they are, how they feel, what they know, what they can accomplish, and where they want to go—leading all people well is getting harder to do. Everything is now blurred in an unintentional tie-dye of responsibility bleeding into increasingly complex patterns.

I longed for the days when there were lines between our personal and work lives, before technology and the nonstop performing it rewards changed that paradigm indefinitely. The outside is in, and all things considered, it's not been good. I've been thinking back to 2020, when the COVID-19 pandemic first hit. No one knew what the next day would bring, never mind the many months to come. People on social media got busy doing what they do: speculating across the entire spectrum of possibility, raising the alarm on everything from an imminent travel ban to martial law. Routines—school, work, appointments, and hobbies—came to a halt as the world scrambled to determine the next best steps toward what would become a very long stretch of confusion, exhaustion, isolation, and unimaginable loss. John and I did our level best to put our six children, three of whom were in (or going to) college and the rest in high school, at ease. But those early days were frightening. And the two years that followed? Brutal.

During this time, network anchors interviewed expert after expert about how our unexpected brush with mortality might change us for the better. Nearly fifteen million people died because of COVID-19 in the first two years of the pandemic. The dramatic loss of life signaled our own fragility, making small things seem smaller and big things seem even more important. The preceding years of greed, materialism, and growing division left many of us in need of a major reset. We were hopeful. Until we weren't. Sadly, COVID-19 was the wake-up call that we, in true egoic fashion, pressed snooze on. We didn't learn much. In fact, we renovated our echo chambers, turned the beds down, and fluffed the pillows.

As I write, each day in America brings news of regression on everything from wealth equality to basic respect. The private sector is emerging as its own battleground, and leaders who identify as helpers are struggling to walk the razor-thin line between their company rules and their own conscience. Today's leadership roles—part psychology, part law, part social work, and part communication—carry immense pressure, and leaders are scrambling to do the jobs they were hired to do while managing dilemmas no one prepared them for. It's untenable.

A conversation with a prospective client brought this into sharp relief. I asked how the growing backlash against diversity, equity, and inclusion had impacted their efforts to create a more inclusive workplace culture. She led DEI for an institution that, for decades, had been considered a guiding light for LGBTQ+ rights. They'd made significant multipronged investments, received widespread recognition, and had an extremely engaged employee resource group whose pride inspired people far beyond company walls. In late 2023, state laws prohibiting gender-affirming care, among other restrictions, forced leaders to reimagine how the company showed up for this community, and while their expressed commitment was the same, their execution was not. Naturally, LGBTQ+ employees and allies were hurt by what appeared to be a decided retreat, turning what had long been a cultural strength into a credibility issue that eroded trust and strained relationships between employer, employees, and community members.

She was rightfully concerned. The institution didn't want to be perceived as abandoning their people, and yet willfully breaking the law put everything they'd achieved at risk. From their perspective, giving a little to keep the lot was a reasonable path forward. But reason is hard to come by these days. This is just one example of the many looming conflicts that both propel and paralyze us. We're afraid to stand still and are equally concerned about moving in the wrong direction.

We were all asking how we achieve workplace safety in an era like this. Is it even possible? And does safety at work matter? Yes. It does. More than ever, we who care enough must create spaces where people can exchange ideas, make mistakes, and challenge assumptions for the good of the business, but also for their own sense of accomplishment. The fact that any experienced leader felt comfortable abandoning these fundamental acts of care was hard to wrap my mind around.

Ultimately, workplaces are microclimates—cultivated spaces within our larger society—where leaders can draw circles of safety around the people they lead. They can show up in ways that help their colleagues and teams feel seen, respected, valued, and protected, even when the outside world is losing its way. And if they succeed in nurturing care and connection among all who exist inside that circle, they don't have to carry the burden of safety alone.

It's possible to achieve this outcome even in the most dramatic circumstances. In early 2022, at the peak of the Russian-Ukrainian war, I was asked to teach human resources professionals in northern Europe my Building Bridges method, which includes respectfully exploring the many emotions and perspectives in the room, then imagining a better path forward together. The company had employees in Russia, Ukraine, and Poland, and uncertainty was high. Everyone was living in fear, and they were processing that fear differently. Some acted out, others shut down, and their relationships—even previously trusting ones—were fragile. Meanwhile, members of the human resources community were dealing with personal trepidation atop a tremendous burden of shared responsibility. They felt called to reduce the harm caused by a conflict they had no power to fix.

No one was sure exactly what to do, but they agreed that creating safety within the team was a start. They wanted to foster a culture of connection—an environment where colleagues could talk to each other with compassion and respect. They wanted genuine relationships to be the norm, not the exception.

I'd been in plenty of high-stakes conversations, but this one felt particularly delicate. I reflected on my very first attempt to use vulnerability to build empathy across differences in a group. It didn't go well.

Early in my consulting journey, I worked with a company that prided itself on its culture, but I knew something was missing. I discovered that while they had a fun and friendly workplace environment (their words), it was not a culture that was recognizing, rewarding, and promoting people equitably. Forty percent of their workforce was comprised of people of color, but 90 percent of its leadership was white, and 70 percent was white and male.

I conducted multiple focus groups and reviewed their employee data. Feeling confident that I'd pinpointed reasons behind the disparities, I jumped right in with the executive team: one Black woman, two white women, and several white men. I asked whether any of them had experienced difficulties related to their visible identities and if they were willing to share.

Silence.

These are the moments when the weight of asking people to be vulnerable hits you between the eyes. In hindsight, I should have known better than to dive right in like that. I didn't remove any of the risk, especially for the one Black woman. I hadn't clearly established the purpose of our time together or set sufficient boundaries. I hadn't allowed the participants to contribute to ground rules. And I didn't create anonymity or ways to discuss topics without any one person having to claim specific issues as their own.

I feel somewhat embarrassed when I reflect on that experience, but I learned a lot from it. This inelegant attempt prompted me to rethink how best to create spaces where participants feel safe sharing their stories and colleagues feel comfortable hearing them. I now know that while in pursuit of higher ground, you must first till the soil.

It was years later that I agreed to speak with the European human resources professionals, and I understood that tensions would be high. There was loss of life, and communities were under daily threat. Differences of opinion were rooted not only in geographical location, but also in fundamental beliefs and values. People empathized with one side or another based on their unique life paths. I spent a lot of time tilling the soil. I wanted to understand the barriers to connection that might surface and be prepared to handle them with care.

What I knew—before stepping foot in the room—was that no one wanted to feel unsafe. No one wanted to feel angry or hurt. No one wanted to believe their colleagues didn't care about them or their feelings. They all wanted the same things, but they believed that opening their minds to another's perspective could compromise their integrity. They were protecting both the validity of their positions and their fundamental value systems. These aren't easy factors to overcome. They strike at the very heart of who we are, or at least how we see ourselves.

I took my time. I asked why they thought we'd come together, what they hoped to achieve, and what ground rules we should establish for everyone's psychological safety—all before we pulled back the veil. Exploring raw emotion in a room filled with people who must work together when they leave that room is a delicate dance. It's important to accommodate the many beliefs and emotions that are likely to show up and to honor—with words and actions—those emotions as markers of a person's current state. From there, it's possible to thoughtfully navigate toward mutual understanding and respect so people can work together more productively. In any emotionally charged discussion, great facilitators create space for everyone to be heard and demonstrate respect for opposing opinions (within reason). Facilitators also learn to be adept at managing real-time conflict and move people toward a clear purpose with a balance of firmness and finesse. Teaching people reliable ways to do this is not easy, but in an increasingly complex work environment, it's crucial.

We had an illuminating conversation. Broke a few barriers. Released a few fears. We didn't fix anything outside those walls in the few hours we were together, but we established something essential to how any group seized by a challenging climate moves forward: a baseline of mutual care and consideration. I give the leaders of this company so much credit for trusting humanity to show up when presented with a new way to invite it. Instead of pointing people to a handbook, they led with humanity.

Especially now, I wanted to do more of this work. It took me back to my professional beginnings at Hallmark, when connection was centered in every strategy, every solution, and every conversation. Susana, a former colleague and forever friend, once said to me while presenting the marketing plan she'd developed to appeal to Hispanic consumers, "People don't care about you until they know you care about them." I remember how encapsulating a thought it was then. Its undeniability still hangs heavy in the air.

This caring connection is both a precursor to safety at work and an outcome. By establishing a clear understanding of how people should treat one another—especially when tensions are high—and holding them accountable for doing so, we relieve ourselves from the position of lone savior. We're no longer single-handedly responsible for fielding every account of wrongdoing, every moment of workplace harm.

Each of us who steps foot in rooms where people are hurting has an opportunity to position a safe, caring, and productive environment as everyone's calling. Creating safety at work is putting people before systems—being *together* before the world.

INTERROGATE YOUR REALITY

I engage with C-suite teams often, and when I do, I reflect on a simple truth: high-level executives rose to their positions by *knowing*, not *wondering*. Teri Ann, one of my former managers at Hallmark, used to encourage us to interrogate our reality. This was her way of reminding us to hold our truths lightly—to understand that what we think we know is a lens and that there's often more than one way to interpret what we see. These days, when it's getting harder to discern facts from fiction, it's more important to be curious than to be certain—to let go of our assurances just long enough to discover something new. The challenge? Not all teams carve out the time for the process of making unconscious thoughts conscious, owning them, setting them down, opening to new thoughts, considering them, and embracing the parts that feel true. This doesn't happen in an hour-long keynote or in the last five minutes of an operations meeting.

I spent a full day with a C-suite team that was mostly male, white, and middle-aged. There were outliers—an older gentleman from Europe who'd been at the company a long time. And three women—one white, one Black, one Hispanic. During our first of many working sessions, I noticed a few things right away. They were kind to each other, and their CEO was clearly purpose driven. While they were focused on the immediate pressures of growing and sustaining their business, there were also hints of legacy thinking in the room. This always encourages me, because leaders who care about lasting impact tend to see connections between situations and people in ways others don't. Some leaders just want to hit their numbers and make their money while managing risk. They're willing to do whatever works in the moment to achieve these goals. Others are focused on the future. They want their positive impact to remain long after they're gone. This leader was focused on the latter.

We came together to lay a foundation for the embedding of workplace inclusion. In my experience, the most successful transformations begin with an engaged executive team. Leaders who don't know a lot about inclusion often make erroneous assumptions about what we do. They expect me to talk about bias. Or race. Or gender. They wait for me to tell them they're doing it wrong—whatever "it" is. But that's not how we at The Waymakers approach the work. We help leaders create conditions, make choices, and exhibit behaviors that allow every single person to contribute fully, freely, and fairly—to thrive in ways that are meaningful to both them and the business. Success means unleashing talent, ideas, collaboration, and results. Those outcomes are achieved by how well we see people and how we respect, value, and protect them. Before leaders can effectively respond to others' views, though, they must first connect with their own.

I shared my "lens" formula with the group: Exposure + Experience = Lens.

"Exposure is what we're taught implicitly or explicitly," I said. "It's what your parents and grandparents told you about people who are not like you. What you saw on television or read about in books. It's what people at church or in the barber shop chatted about during their idle time.

"Experience is what we directly observe or what happens to us and around us. It's the real-world interactions you have with people who are not like you—the meetings, the conversations, the moments, and the memories. Experiences can either reinforce your exposures or counter them. These two elements combine to form the way we see the world and the people in it."

They nodded.

I asked the group to take a few minutes to think about what they were taught about people who are not like them, along with what they experienced, then to consider how their exposures and experiences shape the way they lead. What happened next was by design, but also an encouraging surprise.

One of the men in the group, Alan, shared that he grew up in the Deep South with boldly racist parents and grandparents. He revealed how much it bothers him when people make assumptions about his views based on where he was born. Because he felt so strongly about exposing his own family to more benevolent ideas, he left his hometown as soon as he could and never looked back. As a result of what he'd been exposed to and what he later experienced, he wanted to be the kind of leader who sees people for who they really are.

Jocelyn grew up in a middle-class Black family. Her parents taught her and her siblings that they were capable and worthy—that anything was possible for them. They internalized this view and went on to conquer their corners of the world, one achievement at a time. Jocelyn had experienced her fair share of race-based offenses through the years, as every young Black girl has, but nothing prepared her for what her family faced when they moved into a mostly white neighborhood years later. The vibe was off from the beginning. Some neighbors engaged in silent protest, and others committed escalating offenses until Jocelyn and her husband wondered if it was worth staying. As she relayed this experience, the emotion welled up—not only in Jocelyn, but also in me. She shared this and other instances of feeling disregarded and threatened in places where she was supposed to be safe and where she'd also earned her right to be.

These experiences initiated a conversation about the true

cost of success for professionals of color, which often requires an assimilation into mostly white workplaces, schools, and neighborhoods. What is sacrificed in these transitions? What is gained? And does it balance out in the long run? These are the types of questions being asked in the hearts and minds of Black women all over the country, including me. *Is it worth it? How much is too much for the never good enough on the other side of all this?*

I wondered what the white men in the room were thinking. These were calculations they likely hadn't entertained. For Jocelyn, contributing to a psychologically safe and inclusive environment is paramount, in part because it aligns with her belief system, but also because her experiences have shown her what happens to people's psyche and professional possibilities without it.

Another woman told stories of aspiring to higher levels of leadership while being subjugated at every turn—asked to take notes, tokenized, or given false hope about roles she sought. These experiences were in stark contrast to her exposure, which was rooted in empowerment and advocacy. Her younger years were filled with validation of her potential, but her professional journey challenged those ideas, eroding the confidence she once had.

Perhaps most interesting was the man from Europe, who educated us on caste and the physical danger it creates for those born on the "wrong" side of "right." There are clear lines of demarcation along regional, familial, and religious lines in other parts of the world, with power concentrated accordingly. In these places, your birthright dictates both safety and opportunity. Because of these exposures and experiences, he leads from his head, leaning into what's practical and protective.

We each have our own lens. We can't go back and un-expose ourselves to things we were taught when we were young, but we can broaden that exposure, and we can curate experiences that flip the counterproductive beliefs that separate us and cause us to propagate exclusionary practices.

Our shared experience that day wasn't complicated. In fact, it was extraordinarily human. I simply provided space for the team to reflect on their own life journeys, connect the dots to their current views, and express the hidden thoughts and feelings that influence how they show up. Each person was heard. And each person listened.

This kind of deep personal exploration is not about getting vulnerable for the sake of vulnerability. It's about using reflection as a path to understanding, then understanding as a path to trusting, and trusting as a path to partnering. Reflection and storytelling are powerful learning tools, and in this fast-paced environment, we must be deliberate about making time for it. It just won't happen otherwise.

Leading all people well—whether in an office, a community, or a home—is a faith walk with no end. By facilitating shared understanding and inviting people to rise to the occasion, we can inspire shared commitment. In this way, progress is not a weight resting on one person's shoulders but a group project where all contribute and all benefit. We begin by challenging our assumptions and expanding our views, then moving forward with our earned wisdom in tow.

SEEKING ALIGNMENT

The will and the skill. One of my best friends, Brenda, still tosses this phrase around when we're chatting about situations or relationships that aren't coming together. I first used it years ago when she told me about an ongoing conflict with a manager.

"We know he has the skill," I said to her. "He's been at this a while. But does he have the will? Does he want to support you? Does he care to collaborate with you?"

She didn't know. I explained that some people have the skill—ability, training, knowledge, and experience—to do something differently, but they don't have the will. They don't want to do it. And they're willing to accept the consequences of not doing it because the benefit of staying the same is greater than the benefit of changing. Others have the will but not the skill. They want to change, but they don't know how. In this case, they may be able to learn, but sometimes the learning process is too slow or too difficult. When these two factors aren't present, the relationship won't work.

For helpers, alignment can be a powerful guide. More times than I'd like to admit, I've tried unsuccessfully to make something fit—a project, a hire, or a business deal—because I wanted to be helpful. I felt moved to make a difference. But when there's no alignment in values or priorities, when there's no mutual respect or regard, it just doesn't flow. It's like wrestling with a fish: You're using all your might to eat, and they're using all theirs to live. There's no compromise. Sometimes you both lose, leaving you exhausted and no closer to the catch than when you first picked up the rod.

My good friend Steve had a wife, four young children, and a beautiful house on a wooded lot when he parted ways with his prestigious job. He wasn't fired. He didn't even have a new job lined up. Yet he chose to leave.

Clearly, something had gone terribly wrong.

When he first joined his company, he was excited about the potential. The competitive landscape was wide open, and having led a major market expansion as chief marketing officer elsewhere, he felt well poised to help the organization grow. The new company seemed excited to have him, and it felt like a win-win. Basically, Steve's future was bright…until it wasn't.

Steve and the CEO, to whom he reported, were soon struggling to get into alignment. At first, Steve thought the friction

Leading Through the Wilderness

was over strategy and their differing approaches and philosophies. But as he started to reflect on his short tenure, he characterized the breakdown as something else entirely. His boss did not respect him—or anyone else, for that matter.

Steve had noticed the posturing and bullying behavior right away, although it wasn't directed at him initially. The CEO would yell at Steve's colleagues for minor infractions or throw people under the bus when they weren't in the room. After Steve's first board meeting, just a few months in, when it became clear that the board loved him, his relationship with the CEO changed. His boss began cutting Steve out of important meetings, peeling back his scope of work, and discouraging him from building a personal brand. As an attempt to make his boss more comfortable, Steve went above and beyond to communicate. He was very intentional about sharing information on potential projects. He frequently solicited the CEO's input regarding important decisions. He tried to take advantage of open office time and even attempted to have a courageous conversation about the friction between them but was met with increasing resistance.

Nothing worked. When he discovered the CEO was reorganizing the marketing department in clandestine meetings with his peers, Steve knew he had a real problem.

This was clearly not a healthy relationship, but because there was so much at stake, Steve felt he had to keep pushing through. He was extremely frustrated, increasingly helpless, and a little ashamed. How did he not see this coming? Why would he allow someone—anyone—to treat him this way? And how could he teach his children to stand boldly on their worth if he stayed in a place where his was challenged almost every day?

The day he decided to leave came after an all-out verbal fight in the boardroom. As soon as Steve walked into the meeting, the tension thickened. The CEO began presenting the marketing reorganization. Taken aback but trying to not show it,

Steve challenged an inaccurate statistic. The CEO responded by swearing at him. Steve demanded an apology and would not let the meeting continue without it. The CEO, who was now red and flustered, walked out.

One thing led to another, and within twenty-four hours, Steve had drawn up a memo of resignation. He pulled no punches, ending the letter with a simple: "Write the check, and make it big."

When he first told me this, I couldn't believe it.

"You wrote that down? Just like that?" I asked.

"I absolutely did," he said. "This man had already disrespected me and was threatening my peace. He wasn't going to take from my family too." He never spoke to anyone from that company again.

It's hard to imagine walking away from a C-suite role voluntarily, but as many of us have discovered, some things are more important than money and titles.

When we feel the tension of misalignment, we often wonder if we're just uncomfortable or scared or maybe not giving it our all. People who are wired to give, serve, and be flexible always start with self: *What did I do wrong? Did I not try hard enough?* But it's not always about right or wrong. Sometimes two things just don't fit—you and a company, you and a strategy, you and an employee, you and a volunteer organization, or you and anything or anyone who makes you work harder than the output is worth. We must get better at seeing misalignment earlier and also trusting what we see.

The longer you live, the more you appreciate alignment as a key to greater impact. It maximizes effort. It elevates potential. It opens the door to possibility for all involved and is productive—yielding more energy, more creativity, more joy, and more peace.

We should seek alignment in our circumstances *and* in our relationships—at work, at home, and in the world. Mutually beneficial relationships rooted in respect and consideration are fortresses for helpers and for those being helped. They protect your investments in both directions, giving parties a chance to exchange value, learn from each other, and grow together. Alignment is our friend. When we strive to meet people's needs, they give us more discretionary effort. When we align our values and behaviors, they trust us. When we align our expectations with theirs, people feel clear about how to succeed. And when we align our priorities with their contributions, they feel they're making a difference.

Alignment is one way to ensure your help is purposeful and relevant—that it has the impact you hope it will. That *you* have the impact *you* hope you will. It's the ultimate path of least resistance.

Chapter 10

YOU HAVE TO START WITH THE HEART

Build Bridges

You'd be hard pressed to find a person—beyond a psychologist—more deeply entrenched in the nuances of human relationships than a greeting-card writer. When people first meet me, this is the work experience of mine they're most curious about. They're surprised greeting cards are written by real people. They ask which of my cards was my favorite or the best-selling. They want to know what I studied and how the process works. I explain that being a greeting-card writer is like being an astronomer of feelings. In short, people who specialize in this rare form of writing study the nature, behavior, and composition of human emotion inside the structure and dynamics of relationships and then give language to those emotions. They aim to connect love to love, fear to courage, hope to despair, comfort to sorrow, encouragement to doubt, and joy to celebration. They use carefully chosen words and phrases that inspire people to stop, think, feel, and believe in something greater. Greeting-card writers are, in their own way, doctoral students of the heart—not as a muscle, but as a purveyor of love and all good things.

My corporate career began with greeting-card writing, but it didn't end there. After a couple years writing about everything from breakups to makeups, I became an editor, then an editorial director, then a creative director of editorial, and ultimately vice president of writing and editorial before I moved over to business innovation. While the writing gave meaning to the pieces of our lives, editorial focused on how those pieces fit together. In a company like Hallmark, editing asks us to rise above individual relationship dynamics to design and refine relationship "systems"—networks of emotional needs related to a long list of relationship types and even longer lists of situations, personalities, voices, and sentiments. In practice, this looks like knowing what a brand-new mother might say to her own mother on Mother's Day, having just come to appreciate the depth of love and sacrifice involved in mothering. Or how a person whose husband is a proud provider might celebrate him on Father's Day if he recently lost his job. Or how a brother might reconnect to a sister at Christmas after years of silence. Or how a stepmother might celebrate a child they see as a daughter without using the word *daughter* if it feels a little too soon. The work includes imagining every possible relationship scenario, then seeking patterns, grouping them by themes, and organizing messages that work for each situation specifically and hundreds, if not thousands, universally. It is the very best kind of puzzle.

Over the course of my corporate career, I also created products for and led the development of culturally specific lines for Jewish, Hispanic, Asian, LGBTQ+, and Black communities. Speaking to and for unique communities is a tremendous responsibility. Representing their emotional lives, especially if you don't belong to those communities, means gaining a deep understanding of and respect for multiple realities and caring enough to discover the connections between experiences and expression.

This emotional systems thinking is something that heavily influences our work at The Waymakers. For instance, it's not enough to know how people at work feel. We also want to know why they feel that way, when they feel that way, with whom they feel that way, and how these feelings influence their relationships with their company and work.

A refined ability to dig beneath the surface makes us the ultimate bridge builders. There are four ex-Hallmarkers on my team. This wasn't the plan, but it unfolded this way because we share a critical skill set: we know what great relationships look like, and we understand the very human stuff that lies beneath. The people on my team get what it means to start with the heart.

I served in multiple executive roles during my Hallmark tenure—business, creative, strategy, and culture—and each allowed me to incorporate what I'd learned about relationships into practices that formed community, inspired collaboration, enabled creativity, and unleashed contribution. Leading all people consciously and courageously has always been my "hallmark," and helping others do the same is the simplest way to describe my consulting life.

Leading is the ultimate bridging endeavor. And what is undeniably true today is that we need heart-centered leaders everywhere. Our challenge, especially those of us who identify as helpers, is to learn to lead without losing our footing—to find a way to walk the swaying rope bridge our society has become. To build bridges that don't burn us.

Striving to be before the world has taught me this life-giving lesson: while bridging divides is important, not every chasm is worth crossing. The call to bridge is not an invitation to negotiate nonnegotiables. Some people have deep-seated beliefs that run counter to cross-boundary connection. Some generally good people unconsciously subscribe to ideas that contribute to the erasure or marginalization of others. No one is perfect, and because we're on a continuous learning journey, we can only hope to do better as we know better. But when someone believes they're inherently more valuable than another due to their innate characteristics? When they actively work against the civil rights of their fellow human beings? I will not engage—not anymore. The pursuit of power over progress and control over connection is rampant, and to emotionally avail oneself to this energy is a risk I would not ask anyone to take. This is why I shelved my previous book concept—because bridging can't be about sainthood or self-sacrifice. It's about the meaningful—and dare I say, loving—pursuit of shared humanity.

I now seek to connect with people I can *feel*. People who lead with their hearts, which is apparent in how they interact and spend their time and talents. I don't need them to look like me or come from where I come from. Alignment is a good enough place to begin. By looking for the love in other people and trying my best to lead with the love in me, I've met and am nurturing connections with amazing human beings who keep me believing that we—in binding together our hopes, dreams, gifts, and purposes—are the very bridge between what is and what can be.

SIT DOWN, BE HUMBLE

"You have six children?"

I've seen this look of shock and awe more times than I can count. Parents with three or fewer children, especially young mothers, struggle to wrap their minds around it. They want to know how I survived raising six children, especially as a corporate executive and then as a founder. Parents in blended families have questions about how we approached blending our children, whether the kids get along, if my bonus children like me, and if mine like John.

Blending families can be one of the most challenging parts of remarried life and is the ultimate bridging experience. If you've done it, you know it is a breeding ground for hurt feelings, isolation, claims of unfairness, verbal (and sometimes physical) altercations, and tears. Lots of tears. But while John and I faced the occasional hiccup, we experienced very little friction in our home.

From the beginning, John was very intentional about forming our unit. There was no *yours* and *mine*—only *ours*. If a child came to one of us with complaints about another, he'd tell them to address it directly. If they refused, he'd say, "It must not bother you that much." (Sounds like a personal problem.)

Beyond the unique approaches parenting sometimes requires—not all children are the same—they weren't treated differently based on biological ties. From day one, in John's mind and from his mouth—without flinching—these six children were *ours*. We were a family. And while it took time for their behavior to catch up to our intent, they got there.

They're older now and still a huge part of our life. I've not spoken much about them in this book because they were innocent bystanders during my ups and my downs. That said, some of the most profound bridging lessons I've learned are from them. From the beginning, they insisted on traveling this life path on their own terms and have been generous enough to invite me along.

Kas was in middle school when it first occurred to me that they might be gay. They'd invited a friend over for a sleepover, and the next morning, I found the two young friends sitting side by side at the kitchen island with their pinky fingers intertwined. I didn't say a word, but I wasn't surprised. We had a good relationship, and I trusted they would come to me if indeed there were something to come to me about.

There were early signs that girlhood—with all its frills, pinks, softness, squeals, princesses, and frailty—was not only ill fitting but completely undesirable. Shopping for school clothes was hell. We'd spend hours in the mall, only to leave with a single belt or a couple pairs of socks. My child would rather sit in the dirt and collect rocks and bugs than play with dolls. In fact, I can't recall dolls ever being part of the picture, even though there were plenty lying around. There were no elementary school crushes. No posters of boy bands on the walls. No dreaming of weddings or motherhood. At the time, I thought I had a tomboy on my hands, which I connected to because I was never all that girly either.

Fast-forward to sophomore year in high school. My child became despondent. Irritable. Defiant, even. I couldn't understand why they were so angst-ridden, but I chalked it up to hormones and leaned on every story I ever heard about mother-daughter conflict during the teen years. Everyone had advice to share. *Set this boundary. Take that away. Give it time.* But nothing worked. My child was withering emotionally, and this once-straight-A student began struggling to keep up. It made no sense to me. I did the best I could to stay connected, to show my love, and to avail myself.

Finally, while driving to school one day, they said the thing that had been caught in their throat, in their heart, in their mind, and in their body. They said they didn't want to be a woman (in the traditional sense). My body ran cold, then hot. I didn't know what to say so I chose to respond in the most benign way I could fathom, acutely aware that my response in the moment would either be healing or hurtful. My stomach was in knots. This is not at all what I envisioned.

I hate writing this, but to be honest, I grieved. I grieved for big things, like losing a daughter. But I also grieved for seemingly insignificant things—like the fact that we lived with four boys, my husband, and two male dogs. Was it just me against the testosterone brigade now?

Looking back on this period of transition, I see so clearly what I tried too hard to analyze then: When you must work to be anything other than who you are, you grow weary. You isolate. You feel unsafe. You get depressed. You can't perform. You weigh the pain of being in the world inhibited against the fear of not being here at all. It's not complicated. Each of us needs and deserves to move through this life unburdened—free to be ourselves as long as we're not harming anyone.

Once John and I came to understand what our child needed from us, we became very intentional about providing it—unequivocally—and we demanded the same of our loved ones. Full, unquestionable support was the only acceptable posture. If not that, then nothing. We were prepared to erect a barrier between our child and any person who refused to accept and respect them as they are. *Know what matters.*

Healthy connections between parents and children require an acceptance of who they are, but also overt support for what's important to them. The downside of having six children is your attention is divided. There's no good way around this. You have one body, two hands, one brain, and twenty-four hours in a day. If there are two parents, you can multiply that times two, and it still isn't enough.

Anthony was almost sixteen years old when he appeared to be detaching. John and I consider ourselves generally open and communicative, but also clear about our boundaries, which he was pushing against—hard. I was highly frustrated. I told myself he'd never been much of a talker, so I wasn't surprised that he'd gone quiet, but the resistance felt new.

While sitting in the car one day, I confronted him about his attitude. What came next was an hours-long exchange that began with him declaring he didn't feel we supported his dreams and ended with me in apologetic tears. I had very specific ideas about my parental identity, which included fierce support of my children, barrier removal, endless encouragement, and wise counsel. It was my intent to be a parent who makes a way for my kids to succeed according to their definitions of success. But on this day, it was clear that my impact and my intent were out of sync.

His greatest passion was outside of my knowledge and experience, and it was also high risk. I was so worried about his safety that, according to how he experienced my participation (or lack thereof), I unconsciously withheld my support. I sat and listened as he enumerated the ways I failed to show up for him, each example a dent in my spirit. I could see how significantly my reticence had impacted our connection. He believed I didn't care enough about what he cared most about—and by extension, that I cared less about him than our other children. I was devastated. This was the baby I carried in a sling—across the front of my body—for over a year. The one my friends will never forget because whenever they heard me coming, they saw him first.

I felt embarrassed, and my first reaction was to get defensive. Unwilling to consider a version of myself I didn't like, I tried to justify why I hadn't fully invested. With each rationalization, the distance grew. The space between us was chilly. Indifferent. This was not at all what I wanted.

I silently began talking to myself, and the conversation in my head went like this: *What do you want this relationship to be? How do you want your son to feel? What matters most right now? Is your need to feel right more important than his need to feel supported?*

Focusing on my intent, which was to have a loving, trusting, secure, and enabling connection to my son, helped me move past my feelings of shame and disappointment. Because to be right and good, especially when dealing with those you love, is never the point. *Know what matters.*

The only path forward was to be vulnerably transparent. I told our son that his dream scared me. And that, fear aside, I felt ill equipped to help him. I apologized for withholding my active support. I thanked him for telling me the truth about how he felt and acknowledged how painful it must have been to believe I cared more about his siblings' interests than his or that I somehow believed in them more. And I committed to throwing my weight behind his dream the way I'd done with those before him.

I sat with this for a while, though. I thought I was helping him, but by being hands-off with his high-risk passion, I was really helping myself. It brought me back to my conversation with my friend Melissa, who valiantly overcame breast cancer, and how she insisted on receiving help in ways that would help her—not in ways other people *thought* were helpful. Thinking I was protecting my son, I gave him the opposite of help. I unconsciously signaled unbelief. *Do what counts.*

This conversation gave our relationship a fresh start, but it was just the beginning. I had to show up differently. I had to seek greater understanding about how he felt and what he needed. And I had to keep my promises. I started holding up my end of the bargain, and he became more expressive, which he had vowed to do. Easy? No. Necessary? Absolutely.

As parents, we're supposed to know things—all the things. But this pressure to know—to have the right answers, the right words, and at the right time—extends to any helper. Teachers, doctors, politicians, and leaders feel this pressure every day. In an evolving climate where facts are not truth, this can feel impossible. The pace of change has turned our shared journey on this earth into one big experiment. Expecting ourselves to have a solution to every problem brings out questionable behaviors and separates us from those who desire to co-create with us—to be before the world with us.

Being humble guarantees that we never stop learning. That we can always hear an outside perspective that might enrich our own. That we can create something in partnership with another person instead of being the one holding all the cards. Humility is the position from which we're best suited to heal the brokenness in our relationships and in society at large. What we can't do is keep carrying all the water and getting less to drink.

BE WILLING TO BE WRONG ABOUT PEOPLE

Pretending to read something on my phone, I stood awkwardly on the perimeter of an incredibly diverse and energetic cluster of people who, like me and my son, were waiting for the seminar to start. Some looked at ease and well rested. Others, like they'd just run a marathon. They'd traveled across towns, cities, and states to sort through their goals and their issues. I tried to render myself invisible, hoping to avoid the tall, muscled, mulleted, middle-aged white man with the smirk.

My son and I had arrived in Chicago from Texas earlier that morning. The event hotel was old and weathered. There was one restaurant with a limited menu and odd hours. (No Starbucks in sight.) Hardly anyone was working that day, and the ones who were seemed distracted. As an anxious person, the marked departure from my travel norms made me uneasy, and the span between our arrival and the start of the personal leadership seminar we'd come to attend felt like days.

Waiting for the facilitator to begin, I wondered what I'd gotten myself into. I literally shook my head, trying to shed my negative thinking. This diverse group that spanned experiences, belief systems, and economic stations had gathered for a very specific purpose—to engage in a proven method of unlocking human potential. The experience, the mechanics of which are confidential, included questioning and reframing goals, thought patterns, behaviors, life skills, and relationship habits.

Some participants appeared to be satisfied with their lives and had come to level up. Others were teetering on the edge of hopelessness and came to level out—to rediscover stable ground. I was there because a friend suggested it might help my son build resilience. It wasn't an easy time of year for me to get away, but I hustled the week before so I could go along.

"I know you're attending for your son," my friend said the week prior. "But you might consider what you want to get out of it too."

"Sure, of course," I replied, because it was the considerate thing to say. But I didn't need to get anything out of it. My life was great: happy marriage, thriving business, healthy family, and a beautiful home. I was just going for moral support—or so I thought.

The first activity included introductions. The man with the smirk that I noticed when I first walked into the room that morning was named Peter, and his brief hello reminded me of all the entitled men I'd known through the years who believed their own hype. Who thought their ideas were better, their insights sharper, their work more important. Who, when they couldn't silence you intellectually, would use their physical presence or booming voice to put you in your place. Those who, to this day, step in front of me in the first-class line at the airport, only to have to get up ten minutes later so I can sit beside them. I didn't know him at all. But the seeming arrogance felt familiar, and I had zero interest in dealing with unspoken resistance on my day off.

As divine humor would have it, Peter and I ended up in the same small group. *Oh God*, I thought. I quickly tried to shift my perspective: *You can do this, Tara. Just focus on the possibilities. You're having a human experience. You don't really know this man. He didn't even do anything to you. You're just anxious. Relax.* The self-talk was first rate, but it wasn't working. The only thing that kept me focused was the occasional glance at my son, who seemed to be genuinely engaged.

We ate dinner that evening as a group. As each member voiced their innermost cares and concerns, Peter interjected with his assumptions and overly simplified advice. *What is he even talking about?* My body flushed with heat, but I tried to remain quiet. After all, it wasn't my responsibility to speak for anyone else. Doing so was overtly discouraged. But after Peter's third or fourth ill-timed interruption, I lost it. The comebacks that were stacking up in my head flowed from my mouth like lava. It was, in no uncertain terms, an intervention gone wrong.

"You're putting words in her mouth," I blurted out. "And you're giving advice based on your limited knowledge of her experience. Why can't you just listen?" The table fell silent. I'd been outwardly measured to that point. Ordinarily, the filter between my brain and my mouth is extremely reliable, but not this time. Peter was caught off guard and immediately began defending himself. I don't remember what he said exactly, but it was only a slightly more acceptable version of "I wasn't talking to you." That was true. But while a few members of our group appeared to shrink in his shadow, his vibe had the exact opposite effect on me. *Okay,* I thought. *We're doing this. Let's go.*

"The conversation may not be about me," I replied, "but unfortunately, I have to listen to it. You don't have to say everything you think." The exchange continued for what felt like ten minutes but was probably more like one. "You're sucking the air out of the room," I said to Peter, attempting to put a fine point on a decidedly unrefined conversation. I looked at my group peers, seeking validation. *Surely they see what's happening here?* Nothing. *They must be intimidated,* I thought.

Our group leader, a young man who was heavy on goodheartedness but light on life experience, looked like he'd seen a ghost. He was clearly processing how to regain control of the moment. I watched him, a bit flustered but determined, and felt a twinge of guilt. I certainly didn't mean to make his job difficult. Reluctantly, I relented and leaned back against my chair.

That night, I felt incredibly convicted. Every thought, feeling, assumption, and reaction that came alive in me since laying eyes on Peter was antithetical to who I believed myself to be. As I lay in bed, I struggled to understand why I behaved so badly. Peter hadn't done anything to me personally. All I could come up with was that he appeared to represent so much of what I fight against every day in my work and as a Black woman in the world: Entitlement. Privilege. Brashness. A lack of self-awareness. I realized I may have unfairly burdened him with some of my most challenging human interactions. Facilitating genuine connections across differences is what I do for a living, but in neglecting to pause between thinking and feeling, I'd failed my own test. I know firsthand how powerful genuine connection can be. How enabling. How healing. But in a situation where I felt uncomfortable and frustrated, I clearly forgot.

On the last morning of the seminar, Peter and I were paired for a connecting exercise. Anxious and unsure, I took a deep breath and looked into his eyes as instructed. They were a bright, transparent blue. Like water. And as I'd soon discover, there was indeed an ocean of depth behind them.

I listened to Peter openly respond to the prompt. He talked about his childhood, his work, and his hobbies. He shared some of the areas of his life he was working on and what getting them right would mean to him and his family. He talked about the relationship between his hopes and his fears. In the time it took to actively listen to everything he had to say, my shoulders began to relax. My teeth unclenched. My breath, which had been rapid and shallow, began to slow and expand.

Every challenge Peter shared was some version of a challenge

I'd seen, heard, or experienced: The desire to love and be loved. The need to be seen as good, helpful, and supportive. The balancing act between strength and grace. I knew parts of his story intimately, especially as a parent of young adults—a job no one fully prepares you for that can make you feel surprisingly clueless. Threading the needle between his past traumas, his present instincts, and his future goals was a dance Peter was still learning the steps to. How could he get what he needed while being who others needed? It's a question so many of us have asked ourselves. In fact, I was asking it of myself all weekend.

When it was my turn, I offered Peter what he offered me: candor, vulnerability, and openness. He thoughtfully responded to my story, and his insights were very helpful. It was not what I expected. *He was not who I expected.* The exchange between us released some of the tension that had been building, but it wasn't me who ultimately took the leap. It was Peter.

"I want to apologize for the things I thought about you," he boldly stated later that day. "I was talking to my wife last night, telling her what a [insert popular insult here] I thought you were. I was so turned off by our exchange and made all kinds of assumptions about you and the kind of person you must be. It wasn't fair. I'm sorry."

I didn't see that coming. *You have no idea*, I thought. I'd constructed an entire life story for this man, complete with motivations, relationship dramas, and maybe even a couple rap sheets. I'd taken one look at him, listened to the sound of his voice, watched him in one emotionally charged discussion, and reduced him to the worst of those he reminded me of. In my mind, I accused him of projection, but I was the one projecting—my fears (rejection, judgment, and exclusion) and my hurts (race and gender-based offense, sabotage, and disrespect)—onto him.

I was embarrassed. I apologized in turn and told him the truth, which is that his energy reminded me of people with whom I'd had difficult exchanges and I was triggered. I thanked him for the olive branch and began to see him and his interactions differently from that point on. A few months later, Peter invited my son to stay with him and his family on his next trip to Chicago. The person I assumed Peter to be wouldn't have done that—another reminder of what happens when we assume too much.

We all know Peter. Or at least we think we do. He's the new boss hired from that big-shot company everyone raves about. The seemingly aloof woman just added to our project team. The partner we think wants to take credit for our work. The social media connection who acts like they're better than everyone else. The neighbor who never waves back, even though we're pretty sure she sees us. Every day, we have personal encounters that challenge our patience, our compassion, and our generosity. Every day, the threat to true connection looms large. We weren't designed to live and work like this—waiting for others to disappoint us, or worse. We were designed to benefit from the love, joy, kindness, or support that might be ours if only we were willing to trade our resentment or fear of discomfort for the promise of connection.

I'll be honest. It's hard to hold space for this kind of hope these days. But I have indeed found it when I least expected it. I've learned to cherish even the most mundane experiences that fuel my hope in humanity.

My husband and I spend considerable time in a resort town in Florida. As we were leaving a community event, we noted how every person we met was so *nice*. I realize this sounds like a dumb thing to say, but to be honest, the way political rhetoric is set up these days, we have stopped taking kindness from strangers for granted.

There was the architect and her sister from France, who told us about her family's incredible impact on the area. The Kentucky couple with whom we spoke about our dogs and their idiosyncrasies at length. The Kansas City couple—her from Pittsburgh and

You Have to Start With the Heart

him from Iowa—whom we encountered on our way out. Our connection delightfully delayed our exit and turned into an extended conversation with yet another couple from Baton Rouge about the alligator that likes to sunbathe on the golf course. Random, yes. But a heartening few hours.

That same weekend, our hope was sparked in a retired white man from Alabama who introduced himself to my husband in a furniture store, then sat and talked to him about everything from technology to music for thirty minutes while I shopped. Our hope was sparked again during a brunch we shared with a self-proclaimed "redneck" from Mississippi with whom we became friends after a real estate transaction a few years ago. It was sparked even more in a rural airport as I watched a young white gentleman intervene on behalf of an elderly Black woman who almost missed her flight. And then again as he circled back to tell her how glad he was that she made it. It's not that these interactions change the world. It's that they change *us*, one by one, if we let them. I *will* let them. The alternative is a downward spiral I simply do not want to follow to the end.

These interactions—surprising moments of connection with people who appear to be nothing like us—remind us to remain open. They forge subtle cracks in our defensive walls. When there are multiple experiences like this in a relatively short time frame, the cracks grow wide enough to let the light in. And when that happens, we may feel safe enough to step beyond the threshold.

Not every connection we make will turn into a lifelong friendship, but there is great promise available to us when we realize that separating ourselves from each other out of fear or disdain doesn't keep us safe and that higher relational risk can bring unimaginable rewards.

To state the obvious, some of us are committed to our disconnections. We don't want to be in relationship with a specific person or groups of people, and we have little interest in seeing the humanity in them. We can be committed to our indictments of others for many reasons. Sometimes we think poorly of them because we've not had enough exposure. Sometimes we've had multiple negative experiences that have culminated in us a deep and seemingly immovable distrust. Sometimes seeing the humanity in another person threatens our belief system, contradicting our long-standing position that we are smarter, more capable, or more deserving of love, success, or grace. Sometimes we decide we don't like someone because we believe they don't like us.

I get it. There's enough trauma in the world to last a lifetime, and some of us are hanging on by a thread. We move through our days anticipating the next traumatic event or random act of disregard. We smile outwardly, but inwardly we wait for the person on the other side to take the first step so we can assess their motives and decide if they're worth our effort. It's exhausting. I believe this is where we are today. Uncertain. Unsettled. Untethered. And desperately seeking clarity, assurance, and a reason to believe in something better.

Locking the doors and shutting the windows are reasonable responses to the tsunami of psychological insults accessible to us with a single click or tap. But I remind myself that while social media provides an insane amount of insight and information, I will not find much hope for a more civil society there. I must show up in real life for that.

The truth is that no one gets through this life alone. People need people—it's what separates us from other species. Love and emotional support are requirements for a thriving existence. When we can meet people where they are, value our own well-being enough to sow the care we hope to reap, and seek connection—even in places we believe it doesn't exist—we will not only cultivate more vibrant and successful societies.

We might just save the world.

Conclusion

LEARNING TO BELIEVE AGAIN

Stay Woke

ONE OF MY TEAM members called me the week after Trump's inauguration to tell me about a conversation she overheard between two elderly white women as she walked into the bathroom at her ophthalmologist's office.

"Do you think, now that Trump is president again, he'll make them use separate bathrooms like before?"

My team member shared how she gathered herself, left the bathroom cleaner than she found it, like her mother taught her to (*don't give them any reason to question your humanity*), then walked out and smiled in their faces.

She was incensed but mostly brokenhearted. *They know exactly what this means*, she thought. Unbelievable, and yet so very believable. These moments are why my helper instinct vacillates between healing the land and digging it all up.

My husband and I had a brief exchange about the Oval Office yelling match that broke out between President Trump and President Zelenskyy of Ukraine in late February 2025 and acknowledged that the madness might need to get madder for people to wake up. It's a whirlwind of an era. Some mornings, I take a deep breath and exhale through a full range of emotions. At first, I'm anxious about what may have happened overnight, then angry when I find out. I move through disappointment, then sadness, and by the time I get ready for bed, I feel resigned. To what, I don't know. Like you, I'm witnessing—in real time—the strategic dissolution of our good-faith attempts to realize liberty and justice for all.

Reflecting on every long-term strategy I've ever written, the following vivid scene plays out in my mind:

> There are multiple consumer profiles on easels around a boardroom. A dozen men sit straight-backed in brown leather chairs with their laptops open and glasses of water to the right. For some, it's black coffee. The sun is blinding, and the bearded man at the end of the table rolls his chair backward to the window so he can close the shade. One of the younger men stands to make his pitch. He shares the long-awaited results of his research and outlines the unique concerns and frustrations of multiple segments of the American population.
>
> "Group A," he begins, "feels left behind. They're not succeeding like their parents did. They resent that no one seems to be paying them any attention. They feel overlooked, and we can appeal to their need to feel seen. To be important.
>
> "People in Group B are angry about being painted as the bad guy. We can appeal to their need to feel honorable. We can promise them we'll reinstate the moral and

organizational authority they freely enjoyed before DEI and cancel culture turned them into enemy number one."

There are vigorous head nods around the table.

"People in Group C are split," he continues. "Those who consider themselves traditionalists feel judged by those intent on liberation. Those intent on liberation want to be seen as good people who fight for what's right. We can make this playing field so muddy that they fear moving in any direction. We'll paralyze them and make the few still fighting look insane."

A man near the center of the table chuckles, and the others shoot him a knowing smile.

"Group D? Our biggest threat. They're not only determined and effective mobilizers, but they're trendsetters. Left unchecked, they'll bring people along with them. If we go hard after everything they've worked for, we can break their spirits. Seed hopelessness. Make them stand down."

They're all leaning forward now.

In my imagining, there are a few questions in the room. Some lively debate. The newest member of the task force asks for more evidence, and the presenter shares a montage of Americans of all stripes raging against this and that. There is obvious pain, confusion, frustration, and fear in their voices and in their eyes. He explains that an aggressive campaign with a multifaceted approach can manipulate these emotions to their benefit.

The stout man in the corner who'd been quiet until now but who was an integral part of developing the plan pipes in. "If we come at this from all directions," he says, "we can convince enough American people that DEI is their enemy. Many don't even know what it means, so our definition will be their anchor. Once we establish the anchor, they'll not listen to any other explanation. Combined with other tactics, this will keep them busy fighting for sediment. And while people are distracted by the chaos we create in government and the empty threats we throw at the private sector, we'll execute the plan to grow our wealth and increase our positional power in the world. But we must move with pace."

It's an eerie scene and entirely within reason. Good strategists work with insight. They brainstorm. They identify threats and mitigate them. They resource their plans. They market. They wield language as a light or a sword. They know they must flood the airwaves and that if they do, their version of the truth will dominate.

As someone who began her professional life in product development, I understand that what we're watching is by design. I was mentally prepared for the mind games, but it is even worse than I thought it would be. It doesn't take a visionary to know that the blind pursuit of power, money, and engineered exceptionalism will leave casualties. That all who don't fit the narrowly defined boundaries of Americanness will be left out, cast aside, and erased. But I didn't expect the path to our unraveling to be so swift and unobstructed. It's disorienting. It makes you doubt what you thought you knew. It also makes you doubt what you thought other people knew.

So, what did I think we knew?

I thought we knew that how we treat people who can do nothing for us is a testament to our character. I thought we knew that we reap what we sow. I thought we knew that we are inextricably linked, as Dr. Martin Luther King Jr. wrote in his "Letter From a Birmingham Jail." I thought we knew that God is love—not achievement, pride, control, dehumanization, money, or self-proclaimed superiority.

But we don't appear to know much at all. And to be honest,

I'm not sure it matters. We've moved beyond sensemaking. It's hard to see how we ordinary citizens turn from the self-obsession that led us to cut down those who once stood at our sides and toss them underfoot. In this game of one-upping, there are no winners. If your fellow human being loses, you lose. And if you've been moving through this world believing you are somehow better or more deserving than the next person for any reason at all, you lost a long time ago. (Even if you've gained material things along the way.)

It's complicated. But after sitting with all this for a bit, here's what I believe: I believe the real fight is not about politics, race, age, religion, or geography. I believe these factors are at eye level, and we're grappling with what we can see and most readily understand.

I believe the true fight—if you want to call it that—is between love and apathy, kindness and cruelty, generosity and greed. I believe that while systems govern so much of how we survive, the condition of the heart dictates how we *live*. I believe that we are being called from complacency to consult the deepest parts of us—to uncover what is right and true, apart from the madness and the mandates and the malice. This is the tug I feel in between rolling my eyes and shaking my head. This is what God is seeding in me: the willingness to love anyhow, in the face of the most orchestrated hate campaign I've seen in my lifetime. It's a far cry from Swanson TV dinners, fantasy films with scary puppets, and going home when the streetlights come on.

I believe that we can and should, especially now, ask ourselves the most important question we may ever ask: *Why am I here?* Then, with untamed courage and fierce intentionality, from wherever we are and with whatever we have, *be the answer.*

Being before the world will take a higher level of mindfulness than you've known to date. It means embracing the ideas behind every story in this book. Noticing when you're getting to the end of your own rope and pulling it back from bad actors. Breaking the chains that continue to bind you. Reframing the stories you keep telling yourself that are causing you pain or preventing you from experiencing joy. It means getting serious about your own healing, tending to your wounds, and finding a way to be happy with who you are and what you have, even as you continue learning and growing. It means being deliberate about who you surround yourself with, especially during trying times, and holding fast to your dreams because they have no expiration date that you don't give them. And it means being disciplined in how you use your time and energy so you can accomplish your heart's desires.

By anchoring the *you* in this journey, you make going before others—making a way through the wilderness for those who need help—infinitely easier.

People who have been undervalued by society yet are used for their time and treasures are conditioned to make everything beautiful for everyone else. Without meaning to, and sometimes without knowing it, we settle for the cut stems of the bouquets we lovingly arrange. No more. That house you make is only a home to you when you can stand in any part of it, at any time, and enjoy it the way those you care for do. That workplace only benefits you if you can do the same as the next person and get the same reward. That relationship is only good for you if you get the love you give and, when needed, a little more. The hiding period is over. The suffering by martyrdom is behind us. It's time for us to wake up in the house we've built, open the shades to let the light in, and *live*.

It's Time to Claim Your Inheritance

The last time I spoke to Dr. Maya Angelou was a couple years before she died. I called to update her on the project we'd worked on, and before we hung up, she extended an invitation that hangs heavy on me to this day: "If you ever need my help, please reach out. For anything. Anything at all. You hear?"

"Yes, ma'am. I understand," I replied. "Thank you."

I've not heard her voice since. Not because I didn't need her but because I was afraid I wasn't important enough to call Dr. Maya Angelou—the woman whose work helped shape my own, whose kitchen table I'd dined at, who called Oprah Winfrey daughter and Coretta Scott King sister. I was afraid I didn't have an irrefutably good reason to interrupt whatever extremely important thing she might be doing. Fear anchored me in place, and staying connected didn't feel weighty enough to pull me forward. From my perspective, it was safer to know she cared for me without stress-testing just how much.

In late May 2014, I felt moved to ask a former colleague if Dr. Angelou was okay. They hadn't spoken in weeks, but she promised to check in. A few days later, Maya Angelou—universally beloved thinker, writer, performer—was gone. When she died, those who knew her best lost a mentor. A teacher. A role model. A mother-auntie-sister-friend. But on May 28, 2014, after learning of her passing while cramped in the last row of a Boeing 737, it struck me profoundly that the world lost so much more. Millions of fans who could now say, "I know why the caged bird sings"; who heard "a song flung up to heaven"; who were there "on the pulse of morning"—we all lost a north star who, rooted in the fragile foundation of our shared humanity, consistently and fearlessly pointed us toward our higher selves. She wasn't blindly optimistic, by any means. She lived through Jim Crow and the civil rights movement. She was friend to Malcolm, Martin, Baldwin, and Hughes. She was a warrior for justice and an unapologetic believer that Spirit is with us, for us, and in us. She wielded hope like a shield and love like a sword. There were none before her—self-made women who bridged pain and promise so effortlessly. There have been few since.

The news of Dr. Angelou's passing made me feel less sure of myself. Hers was the wisdom that watered many seeds of greatness in me.

There was the time I stood to offer the chair opposite her to a man I clearly thought deserved it more. She lowered me with her gaze. "Sit," she instructed. "You're just as worthy of that seat as anyone." *Claim your space.*

And the day in Santa Monica when she stopped mid stride to correct a young woman who ran toward her screaming "Maya!" from across the street. *Respect. Composure. Safety.*

There was also the brisk but sunny afternoon we sat around her dining table in Winston-Salem, North Carolina, marveling at the many works of art displayed throughout her home. "If it's not beautiful or useful," she advised, "get rid of it." *Inspiration balanced with function.*

And most meaningfully, the ways she taught me to value my own expertise each time she graciously received editorial guidance from me, which is how our relationship began. There is no greater compliment than to have your talent—your creative judgment—recognized by someone you've admired since childhood and whose work is the standard bearer in your field. *You are worthy.*

In my hand, I'd hold the yellow legal pad filled with original sentiments written in her hand. I'd search her words for relevance to birthdays, anniversaries, holidays, encouragement, congratulations, and gratitude. When the connections were clear in my mind, I would pick up the phone to discuss approvals and suggest edits.

"Hello, Dr. Maya Angelou's office," her beautiful, kind associate would answer.

"Hi, this is Tara at Hallmark. I'm calling for my meeting with Dr. Angelou."

"Hi, Tara! Hold on one moment, please."

Learning to Believe Again

A few minutes later—a warm, lyrical "Hello, dear."

"Good morning, Dr. Angelou. I'm calling to talk about the writing you sent me."

"Yes," she would affirm. "Let's!"

Our editing sessions were iterative: "What about this word?" "How would you feel if we moved this last line to the top?" "I'm not sure we need this part...you captured the same idea so memorably in the second line."

Sometimes she pushed back. "No, that doesn't mean the same thing. What I'm trying to say is...," and she'd offer an alternative. Other times it would click, and I could hear the smile in her response. "Yessssss. That's it! I like it," she'd say, each syllable elongated. If you ever talked to Dr. Angelou on the phone, you know that you could hear her smiling.

I was a mere twenty-five years old when these conversations began, and I encountered each with amazement. There was never a time I wasn't afraid I'd overstep, but it was my job to translate her brilliance into a version of itself I happened to be more expert in. Deep breaths before, then nerves—and afterward, overwhelming gratitude.

In the decade we worked together, there were countless memorable moments—professional and personal. Dr. Angelou sent flowers for the births of my children and made me a vanilla cake from scratch when I turned thirty. In her presence, time passed slowly. We didn't just share meals; we shared bites of storied dishes lovingly prepared. We didn't just listen to her memories; we experienced the humor, love, and courage in each step of many small journeys that, together, made a beautiful, vibrant, history-altering life. How fortunate to have known a living legend. How formidable this magnificent void.

Over and again, I've wondered what might be different about society if she were still here. What would she write about now? What would she say about the banning of her books—each its own masterpiece and, together, a master class? I wonder what she and Ms. Winfrey would discuss in television interviews or podcasts. How she would reframe both our human challenge and our leadership opportunity in this precarious moment, when walls are erected daily, chasms are rapidly expanding, despair is taking root, and our way forward as a human race feels less like an open road and more like one massive stumbling block.

Dr. Angelou became an ancestor more than ten years ago, and while it intimidates me to write this in a way I can't erase, I've often felt called to build upon her legacy—to use curiosity, love, and language to illuminate our dark corners and to lighten the psychological loads of those who have been denied the joy that is their birthright.

Dr. Maya Angelou signed her books "Joy!" When I first saw it on the page, I received it as a mandate. Joy! in the face of resistance. Joy! beyond perceived limitations. Joy! in the proverbial darkness. Always and in all things: Joy!

I intuitively knew that by signing her work this way, she was inviting every reader to cultivate joy when it lay dormant, to create joy when it was absent, to preserve joy when it was under threat, and to amplify joy wherever it lived. I was sure she'd written the word a thousand times, and I was just as sure no one could possibly mean it as intently as a Black American woman in her seventies who'd traveled as far and overcome as much and loved as freely as she had. Everything Dr. Angelou said and did was imbued with passion and purpose.

I believe we each have an inheritance. We have God-granted gifts—ways our minds, hands, mouths, and bodies work—that are unique to us. We've had exposures and experiences that have shaped us. Beliefs that anchor us. A purpose that fuels us. Community—people who were sent to love, support, guide, and watch over us. Voids we were designed to fill but not lose ourselves in.

Learning to Believe Again

After my healing and light language session in DC with Kimberly, after which she told me I was a visionary, she paused to emphasize a point. "You have help," she said, nodding her head.

"Where did that come from?" I asked. I was curious about why she said that at that moment and in that way.

"I can see them," she said. "They are here." Her eyes scanned the space around my body. "You just have to call them."

I was immediately reduced to sobs. I knew exactly what—and who—she saw.

Dr. Angelou believed that every time she stood to speak or teach, her ancestors were in the room, cheering her on. That they followed her up to the stage, shouting, "Yes!" She would often declare, "I come as one, but I stand as ten thousand." In a speech honoring the opening of the National Museum of African American History and Culture, while talking about calling on the ancestors, Oprah Winfrey said, "I've never been anywhere God didn't want me to be." We are never alone. And you are, as you read this, exactly where you belong.

I believe we are the answer we've been waiting for. Each of us and all of us—the invisible, forgotten, uncertain, and seemingly hopeless who are just scared, lost, or alone. We are our sanctuary. There is nothing we can't achieve if we determine to love one another in it and through it.

I believe Dr. Angelou is with us still and that she would want us to be both brave and whole. I believe she would want us to follow our passions and fulfill our purposes and not take no for an answer. And I believe she would expect us—with our inheritance in tow—to show up for each other every step of the way. To be before the world…as one.

Keep the Faith

I didn't grow up in the church. Over the years, I've heard Spelman sisters, colleagues, sorority sisters, and clients speak about long days sitting in pews, begging for butterscotch candy from their seatmate's purse bounty, being read the gospel at their grandmother's knee, attending Vacation Bible School every summer and children's Bible study every Sunday.

They say they met their first friends at church. That they were raised by a community of elders who served as surrogate parents and aunts and uncles. That they prayed before every meal and every night as they prepared for bed. They say this belief—that there is a God who loves them, watches over them, and orders their steps—has been the foundation of their comfort and confidence for as long as they can remember. That they have never doubted—through storms, loss, and setbacks—that God would provide.

As a child, my brush with faith was brief and complicated. The local Catholic church where I grew up refused to bury my paternal grandfather because he'd been divorced, and my father held this against them—the priests who ordered it and the principles on which their decision stood. My maternal grandmother used to pray the rosaries with me, but I was more interested in the beads and poeticism than the meaning of either.

I was a senior in high school when I had my first personal encounter with God. My best friend invited me to a small service on her college campus, where fifteen or so had gathered to praise and worship. I went not because I felt compelled but because she invited me. In a series of events that are fuzzy now, I was brought to my knees. The best way to describe the impact of this experience is to say that I felt less alone. Less unwanted. Less unseen. More held. More purposed. I felt part of something greater, and I wanted to continue feeling that way. In the years that followed, I called myself Christian and had moments of extreme closeness with God. I also had disassociated moments, like the ones I mentioned earlier. But even when I felt far from the systems that purported to uphold Christianity, I still believed there was a God.

It wasn't until the divorce and my restoration period that I understood firsthand the reality of divine orchestration. The God winks I referenced in chapter 3 were undeniable.

In late 2007, I attended a sister circle where one member shared a prayer that changed everything for her:

> Dear God, please remove from me any person, place, or thing that *is not* part of your divine plan for my life. And God, please bring unto me any person, place, or thing that *is* part of your divine plan for my life.

She warned us not to pray this prayer until we were ready for things to fall apart. She explained how everyone she knew who prayed it went through a painful transformation process but was exceedingly blessed on the other side. I was already miserable. I knew it was a prayer I should pray, but a few days passed before I spoke those words. I had to gather my courage first.

In a matter of weeks, my marriage descended into chaos. As you now know, this was every bit as painful as our sister warned it would be. But God!

God winked when I found the photos and videos.

God winked when the preacher on the television spoke the words I most needed to hear about not going back.

God winked as I watched *Nights in Rodanthe* and when Diane Lane's character, Adrienne, told her daughter, "There's a kind of love that makes you feel anything is possible; I want you to know you can have that."

God winked when my bonus was almost the exact dollar

amount needed to erase the real estate debt incurred by my ex-husband, days after I fell to my knees crying out for help.

God winked when my friend asked me to write a letter asking for what I wanted in a husband, and God winked when my current husband, John, was delivered.

God winked when my and John's custody schedules lined up to a tee, allowing us to spend time together although we each had three children.

God winked when, because it was the Saturday of all our children's spring breaks in different cities, I married John on 3:16... *for God so loved the world.*

God winked when the stone I picked up from the pile of soil and rock became the site of our family home.

God winked when the job I left became the business I built.

God winked when I came across voices and views that finally made sense to me—that reinforced a God of universal love, not judgment, condemnation, leverage, pride, or greed.

God winked when I set aside the book I thought I wanted to write for the book I was called to write—the one you're reading now.

God keeps winking at me in every moment of protection, overcoming, understanding, abundance, and peace amid overwhelming unrest. When people ask me why I believe, the answer is simple: *I have seen the goodness of God.*

I do not believe God is in the actions that unfolded leading up to and that have persisted since the election. I do not believe God is in school raids, fiefdom, bigotry, lawlessness, idolatry, and hatred. I do not believe God is in marginalization, inequity, dehumanization, and war. I believe God is love. I believe God is help. And I believe that when God chose us in Him before the creation of the world, it was to be the both the purveyors and recipients of that love and the reason for that help.

God also winked when Socrates showed up at the door the

first time—and then months later, when I returned to Florida. Again I ordered groceries, and again his name popped up in my app.

Since I'd seen him last, I'd worked with our team designer, Erica, to make art from life. His "You are before the world" reminder had such an impact on me that I'd asked her to create a design to put on a postcard and a sweatshirt. I then posted on LinkedIn that I would send fifty Black women (the 92 percent) a gift for the holidays and asked that they email me with their shirt size and mailing address. Erica nailed the design on the first go and helped get the sweatshirts made. Kaylin, our operations manager, who is also my beloved niece, generated a spreadsheet with everyone's names and information. My oldest son, Abram, packed each gift neatly in its mailing envelope, and Kaylin sent them to their new homes. It felt good to use my creativity to shine a light in what I felt was a dark time.

In the beginning, I thought the "You are before the world" moment would remain exactly that—a moment. But one night a voice kept waking me: *You are before the world. You are before the world. You are before the world.* I'd written about my encounter in one small chapter of what was the previous draft, which I'd titled *See the Light*, but in my dream state, the piece became the whole. When I woke, I knew that this phrase Socrates unassumingly dropped on me was so much more.

It was God lovingly reminding me that I am always held and guided, sufficient, and worthy of care.

It was God prompting me to go before—to bring the gift of worth and loving boundaries to others who were also weary but refused to be worn.

And it was God challenging to me to start with people. While my work has been systems focused, it was time for me to practice what I preach—to speak to the hearts of people instead of being distracted by our representatives, gimmicks and games, or worldly pursuits.

I changed the framing of this book that day. In sharing with you the many ways I've learned and am still learning to be before the world, I hope to offer you what others have offered me: a mirror. A place to see the beauty in the ashes. A way to shine the light on your own rebirth and to also bring the rain. None of this is easy or clean. It can be nasty work. But we deserve to fill the spaces we create. It's past time to sit at the tables we set as our true selves and not the carefully constructed versions we parade in public.

The completion of *You Are Before the World* coincided with the last of our children leaving the nest. The morning after he moved out, I walked up the stairs and turned to the west side of the house to look for something. On the wall between the bedrooms that were home to our middle sons hang six photos of our children, arranged by birth order. They were between three and eleven years old when the photos were taken. I stopped to gaze at each one, their personalities evident even then. Ja'Nae, strong and determined. Kas, intellectual and intuitive. Abram, reflective and compassionate. Christopher, confident and adventurous. Anthony, curious and witty. Chase, observant and responsible. Six incredible human beings, each with unique stories and talents and interests. They've changed me from the inside out. They've made me a better person, opening my heart and my mind to new ways of thinking about the world.

I walked into Christopher's old room to see a naked mattress. No trophies or ribbons or photos. No clothes or stuffed animals. No vision boards. I backtracked to Abram's room to find a few loose ends he planned to come back for—his keyboard, a television, and a humidifier. Anthony's old room is now my office. It's filled with artwork, books, my desk, and a couch with vibrant pillows. A flip chart and a money tree. Chase's room was empty now too. A couple ribbons hung on the wall, and an old gift bag from his grandmother that undoubtedly held lotion and bath wash sat on the bathroom vanity. Our oldest two had been gone for a while.

Standing in the common area of a space that belonged wholly to them, it rose up in me—the sadness. People always say your kids grow up too fast. While you're carting people to practices, after-school meetings, and open houses, you don't believe them. In fact, you sometimes secretly hope for an end to the intensity that is raising more children than you have hands and feet.

Until they leave. And you know you've turned a page.

Almost immediately, John and I began transforming Chase's room into a cardio room. John had ordered foam squares for the floor. We each had a stack, and as we placed the squares in their spots, interlocking the edges to create a new surface, I was reminded of when we first moved in a decade prior. John and I spent sixteen hours a day over two days putting together no fewer than ten pieces of IKEA furniture. Screw by screw, we built our children's dressers, nightstands, bookshelves, and tables. If you've ever assembled IKEA furniture, you know there are no written instructions—just pictures in the order of assembly. Successfully collaborating on this task with minimal restarting requires extreme communication. As John and I neared the end of that first major group project, I'd poured us each a glass of wine and laid out some snacks. When we finished, we joked about how the exercise was proof our partnership was destined to last.

We relished our new beginning and couldn't wait for the children to see what we had made. Now, more than a decade later, with foam squares in hand and empty bedrooms echoing my emotion back to me, it felt like an ending. The days in front of us would be so different from the days behind us. I knew this was a good thing and felt excited about our future, but I also felt the pulsating magnitude of the loss.

Just then, the phone chimed. It was Ja'Nae. She'd arrived at the hospital where, hours later, she would give birth to our second grandchild, a baby brother to our first grandchild, Grace. God's timing is impeccable. I laughed out loud, then silently remembered what fifty years have taught me several times over: no matter how bad things may seem on the surface, new life is always on the way.

Afterword
A HOPE AND A FUTURE

We dig in deep and toss our care
into the crisp and thinning air around us.
It's still dark and the ground's still dry.
It should be lighter now.

We planted seeds and watered them.
Removed the weeds beneath the stem that bound us.
They're still there. And they're growing high.
We say we don't know how.

Both rain and fire, too damp and hot—
a threat to soil and yield. The rot, it found us.
We pray we've not lost all the rye—
A symbol. Hope. A vow.

We're foraging for remnants here,
but they'll not be uncovered where they drowned us.
We'll need to find new land and sky.
To sow new dreams. To plow.

True love is never lost to time.
We mourn, we sing, we paint, and rhyme to ground us,
then stretch to pull each other nigh…
to mend the breaking bough.

—TARA JAYE FRANK

RESOURCES

PART I
YOU: BE STILL AND KNOW

CHAPTER 1: HOW DO WE STEADY THIS VESSEL?

- *Inclusion Uncomplicated*, Dr. Nika White
- *Sisterhood Heals*, Dr. Joy Harden Bradford
- *Rest Is Resistance*, Tricia Hersey

CHAPTER 2: IT'S TIME TO LOOK DEEPER

- *The Waymakers*, Tara Jaye Frank
- *The Hate U Give*, Angie Thomas
- Ener-ki, Reiki master and shaman, www.ener-ki.com

Acceptance: *Ninety-Two: The Silent Revolt No One Saw Coming*, documentary by Dr. Jade Singleton

PART II
ARE: TAKE CARE OF YOURSELF FIRST

CHAPTER 3: HOW DO I CHOOSE MYSELF?

- "Goodness of God," CeCe Winans
- *Testimony: Vol. 1 (2006)*, India.Arie
- *The Shack*, William P. Young

CHAPTER 4: SAY GOODBYE TO SELF-SABOTAGE

- *The Seven Spiritual Laws of Success*, Deepak Chopra
- *Unlearning Silence*, Elaine Lin Hering
- EMDR Therapy, emdria.org

CHAPTER 5: RESTORATION

- *The Value in the Valley*, Iyanla Vanzant
- *Testimony: Vol. 2 (2009)*, India.Arie
- *Power Moves*, Sarah Jakes Roberts

CHAPTER 6: GETTING FREE

- *In Search of Our Mothers' Gardens*, Alice Walker
- *Drama Free*, Nedra Glover Tawwab
- *We've Got This*, Ritu Bhasin

Comfort: www.alexisgiftquilts.com

PART III
BEFORE: CLEAR A PATH FOR OTHERS TO FOLLOW

CHAPTER 7: EMERGING

- *Things I Should Have Told My Daughter*, Pearl Cleage
- *Build the Damn Thing*, Kathryn Finney
- *I Came to Slay*, Elizabeth Leiba

CHAPTER 8: GROWING UP

- *It's About Time*, Valorie Burton
- *Set Boundaries, Find Peace*, Nedra Glover Tawwab
- *Speak*, Tunde Oyeneyin

Community: www.therapyforblackgirls.com

Part IV
The World: People Are More Important Than Systems

Chapter 9: Leading Through the Wilderness

- *The Color of Emotional Intelligence*, Farah Harris
- *All About Love*, bell hooks
- *The First, The Few, The Only*, Deepa Purushothaman

Chapter 10: You Have to Start with the Heart

- *Matters of the Heart*, Dr. Thema Bryant
- *The Universal Christ*, Richard Rohr
- *Talk to Me Nice*, Minda Harts

Conclusion: Learning to Believe Again

- *Wake Up America*, by Keisha N. Blain
- *Maya Angelou: The Poetry of Living*, Margaret Courtney-Clarke
- *Black Liturgies*, Cole Arthur Riley

Courage: www.thelovelandfoundation.org

ACKNOWLEDGMENTS

Writing *You Are Before the World* has been, as previously mentioned, an act of obedience. My first thanks are to God for trusting me with these words and ideas and for granting me both the edifying and corrective experiences that gave them meaning.

In the beginning…

Thank you to my parents, who showed me how to be truly human and who always encouraged me to be myself in a world that wants desperately to constrain us.

Thank you to my Tetea, who thought me "special" and deserving all along and who is still with me in spirit every day.

Thank you to my brothers, "sisters," aunts, uncles, and cousins, who love me without condition and who always wish me happiness.

In the darkness…

Thank you to Melissa, Brenda, and Ron, who knew more than anyone about my first darkness and who were also present at first light.

My Spelman Sisters, who offered to ride for me in ways I will not write down so they can stay free.

My other "Sisters in the Circle," who regularly modeled care, support, and joy.

To Jen, who pulled me out of a particular ditch, and Lindsey, who helped brushed me off.

To Callie and Torrance, whose home and friendship were a sanctuary when I was losing my mind.

To my Hallmark colleagues, including my teams, and Tammy, Ellen, Dave, Ann, Susana, Marquetta, Pete, and many more who—unbeknownst to them—provided the very best kind of distraction when I needed it most.

Thanks to Chris and Reggie, who stayed up late to talk me off countless ledges. Rest in heaven, Reg.

And to Dr. Angelou for loving me and believing in me. You are missed.

First light...

Thank you to Dr. Alduan Tartt, who advised me to write the letter that changed my life and the lives of our entire family.

To my children—all of them—whose insistence on defining success on their terms make the concept of true freedom easier to grasp every day.

My deepest gratitude to the love of my life and spiritual partner, John, for supporting my need to process my life story in this way and for being a wise and willing participant in every chapter. And to his parents and sister, who are—in every way that matters—my own.

Learning...

Thank you to Keith for mentoring me on everything from capturing business value to riding the wave of entrepreneurship. Your friendship means the world to me and John.

Jacque, Machelle, Keriann, Trudy, Jo, Mike H., Mike U., Em—thank you for helping, teaching, connecting, creating, and supporting as I learned to build a company.

To Meghan and Blair—I appreciate the bridge.

To my team—Kimberly P., Kaylin, Erica, Teresa, Fay, Aminah, John, Lori, and others—whose insight and expertise help us help others lead all people well.

And to my LinkedIn community—especially my early readers—who generously validated that I was on to something good and important.

Acknowledgments

Growing…

Thank you to Richard Rohr. Your voice and work have helped me find my spiritual home.

Thank you to my author sisters for walking this road alongside me with your hands at my back.

Thank you to Jevon Bolden, my agent, who believed in me and in this book, and who—with her talented team at Embolden Media Group—helped make it possible for you to hold it in your hands.

Leah Lakins, you are the truth! Thank you for sharpening my pen.

Thank you, Kimberly Dawkins Bargassé. Your gift arrived in my life right on time.

Thanks also to Jade, my twin eagle. Your vision helps me see my own more clearly.

And, finally, I offer my undying gratitude to Black women, who continue to show up with open hearts and hands, even as we are undercut and underestimated. May we keep learning to be before the world…together. This book is for you.